How to
Start and Run
Your Business
THE RIGHT WAY

How to Start and Run Your Business

THE RIGHT WAY

A Guide to Protecting You and Your Business from Lawsuits and Audits

Michael B. Bowman, Esq.

ANDERSON
LEGAL, BUSINESS & TAX ADVISORS

DISCLAIMER

This book is intended to be informative and to aid in the education
of its audience. It is sold with the understanding that neither the
author nor the publisher is engaged in rendering legal, accounting,
financial, or other professional advice. As each individual
situation is unique, questions specific to your circumstances
should be addressed to an appropriate professional to ensure that
your situation has been evaluated carefully and appropriately.
The author and the publisher specifically disclaim any liability or
loss incurred as a consequence, directly or indirectly, or using
and applying any of the concepts of this book.

I dedicate this book to my family and my business partners. Without their support I would not have been in the position or have the passion to help others with their businesses. To all who read this, I wish you the best of success in your lives and in your businesses!

Contents

1

The Risks of Small Business Ownership

I magine having sacrificed long hours and plenty of hard-earned money to create and foster a successful business. You've left the rat race, developed a stable and respectable income for yourself, and created a legacy for your family. Now imagine, out of the blue, being served papers listing your business as a defendant in a lawsuit and subsequently watching that one gut-wrenching moment snowball into the heartbreaking loss of your business, your personal assets, and everything you've ever worked for. All of it gone, taken through the court system, just like that.

It happens all the time in the United States. And far too often it happens to small business owners who thought that they had done everything right.

Many people are under the false assumption that if you simply file your business as a corporation, LLC, or limited partnership, the law will automatically protect you personally from a lawsuit against your business. Unfortunately, it's a little bit more complicated than that.

Lawsuits by the Numbers

It's estimated that 90 percent of all small businesses are involved in a lawsuit at some point during their existence; 90 percent! In any given year, between 36 and 53 percent of all operating businesses are involved in a court proceeding or trial[1]. Of those cases in which a lawsuit is specifically filed *against* a small business and its owners, roughly 40 percent of them will have their corporate veils "lifted" or pierced by the courts[2].

It sounds absolutely terrifying but what does this all mean?

It means that your business is probably going to be sued at some point. And if you don't file and operate the business legally and properly, your business *and* your personal assets will both be at risk.

The good news is it doesn't have to be that way and it certainly shouldn't deter you from following your business dreams.

The Shotgun Method

I can't tell you that you can avoid lawsuits, altogether, because the truth is that we live in a lawsuit-crazed society.

1 Rubin, Basha. "You're Going To Get Sued—Here's How Not To Get Screwed." *Forbes*, 14 Jul. 2014, www.forbes.com/sites/basharubin/2014/07/14/youre-going-to-get-sued/#23b7889c7f08.

2 Thomas K. Cheng. "The Corporate Veil Doctrine Revisited: A Comparative Study of the English and the U.S. Corporate Veil Doctrines," *Boston College International and Comparative Law Review*, 1 May 2011, lawdigitalcommons.bc.edu/iclr/vol34/iss2/2.

Everybody is looking to the court system for help or an easy payout, and the lawyers certainly don't make matters any better. Far too many litigation attorneys use what I call "The Shotgun Method." Their clients come to them with grievances, complaints, or losses, and the attorneys' job is to represent them, restore them, and "show them the money." Rather than looking for the actual cause of the wrong done to their clients, they simply list every defendant possible. Anybody with money or assets who is even remotely close to the situation is fair game. Often, this means small businesses and owners with other assets. Then, they make "generous" offers to the defendants to settle out of court. The defendants have few other options available because fighting the cases in court could actually cost them even more than the settlements. So they settle and agree to pay for something they likely had nothing to do with or no control over in the first place. It essentially amounts to a hostage or extortion situation, and it happens every single day in the American legal system.

These are realities that we simply can't avoid or control.

However, what I can tell you is how to establish, maintain, and run your small business so that the risk of lawsuits is minimized and, if your business does get sued, it doesn't lead to the piercing of your coveted corporate veil.

What Is the Corporate Veil and Why Is It So Important?

Imagine that there's a giant legal curtain separating your business assets and activities from your personal assets and life. Although thin, this curtain is a critical dividing line that shows where you end and where your business begins. This is your corporate veil, and it should not be crossed, pulled up, or opened for any reason. If you break this cardinal rule and start slipping things under the curtain—money, activities, debts, agreements, etc.—you're failing to act in a "businesslike manner." You're blurring the line between yourself and your business.

If your business were to be named as a defendant in a lawsuit, by a creditor, employee, client, customer, or even bystander, a shotgun attorney is going to pull every public record on you and your business that he can possibly find.

If he sees any indication that you've been slipping things under the curtain and blurring those lines, he'll see a chance to prove that you've been failing to act like a legitimate and proper business. If the court agrees, a judge can pierce or lift that corporate veil, which is the same as saying, "There is no business—only a person." Your corporate protection will be stripped entirely, and the plaintiff's attorney will have free rein to dig into your personal life and assets and go after anything he can find. In other words, instead of taking your business down, the shotgun attorney will take *you* down.

We'll go into specifics and details throughout this book but understand, for now, that if you fail to keep your personal and business activities clearly separated by that veil, any formal entity protection can be negated, your curtain of protection can be lifted, and everything you personally own could be up for grabs in a lawsuit.

Audits and the Corporate Veil

It's important to note here that lawsuits are not the only path that can lead to the piercing of your corporate veil. IRS audits can be a culprit as well, and although audit rates have dropped in recent years, it's still a possibility that shouldn't be ignored or overlooked.

The IRS Code specifically allows the government to pierce the corporate veil if the IRS finds that "trust fund taxes" have not been fully paid by the business or if your accounting procedures show that you've been failing to maintain that clear separation between yourself and your business. Even though 2014 audit rates for business filers (the latest numbers available) were only between .04 and 12.2 percent (depending on the filing type)[3], the reality is that an IRS audit can also lead to the piercing of your corporate veil and more trouble than anybody ever wants from the IRS and its courts.

I Wish I Would Have Met You Sooner

Over the course of my career, I've met countless people who said, "I wish I would have met you sooner," because, unfortunately, they had lost their businesses and personal assets when their corporate veils were pierced.

The only way to avoid these situations is to make sure that you treat your business as a business from day one,

3 United States Department of the Treasury, Internal Revenue Service. *2014 Internal Revenue Service Data Book,* 1 Oct. 2013 to 30 Sept. 2014, www.irs.gov/pub/irs-soi/14databk.pdf.

and isolate it from your personal activities by respecting the division created by your corporate curtain, or veil. Never forget that a business entity is a separate being from you personally, not an extension, and it must always be treated as such.

Some accountants and attorneys will tell you that this is a lot of work and a really big hassle. The truth is that it's simply a matter of keeping accurate records, separating the business finances from your personal finances, and clearly entering into business transactions as the business and not the individual. It's entirely possible to accomplish all this and worth every bit of effort it may take.

The information contained in this book is vital to keeping your personal assets safe from your business activities and maintaining the integrity of your corporate veil. *That's* what this book is all about, and *that's* why it's so important.

2

How the Corporate Veil Works

Technicalities

Sole proprietorships and partnerships do not create a clear separation between you, as the business owner, and your actual business, because there is no legal affirmation establishing that you and your business are two separate beings. By all accounts, you are one and the same. That's why these types of business formations will never provide the protection of a corporate veil. By definition, they can't. What you need (although there are exceptions) is a "stand-alone" entity. The concept of stand-alone entities can be traced all the way back to the Roman Empire, so they're deeply rooted in our legal system and ideals, and have long withstood the test of time.

Formal, stand-alone entities, such as corporations and LLCs, are separate beings in the eyes of the law because they are created and born by filing organizational documents with the secretary of state. (More on that process later!) The law treats corporations and LLCs as distinct and autonomous entities that are created, or born, on the date of their filing. Just as a U.S. citizen gets a birth certificate at birth, a formally filed business entity receives a certificate of existence that is granted by the secretary of state when the entity is officially filed.

Because corporations and LLCs are independent entities, they have rules, boundaries, and legally enforceable rights, just like you and me. They can acquire debts, own property, and generate profits. They have the ability to enter into and enforce legally binding contracts, separate and apart from their owners and managers. And, since these entities are independent beings, they are also required to file and pay taxes on any profits generated by their business activities.

The legal, formal business formation of a corporation or LLC is what officially creates your corporate veil—the critical dividing line that clearly shows where you end and where your business begins. This concept is meant to encourage entrepreneurs to take chances and risks in the business world. Without this protection, how many of us would really take the plunge? And of those who do risk small business ownership without the proper formalities and curtain, most end up regretting it.

Keep in mind, however, that the corporate veil limits your loss to the personal investment you made in the business. For example, if you personally invest $50,000 into your business and the business gets sued and loses in court or goes bankrupt, you will lose your original $50,000 investment, but your personal assets will remain sheltered and protected.

The bottom line is that when a corporate veil is created and well maintained, the business will be responsible for its own debts and liabilities, and your personal assets and accounts will generally be off-limits to creditors and courts. (Of course, there are exceptions, and we'll discuss those throughout the book.)

Directors, Officers, Members, and Managers

When you formally file your business entity, you'll need to choose and select a team to run your business. Depending on which type of entity you form, and how large or small your business is, your team may consist of a dozen people or just you. Either way, if filed, respected, and properly maintained, your business entity will protect not only you, but also any other owners or partners, as well as the officers, directors, and members, of your LLC or corporation. They'll all be protected against legal actions taken by third parties against the business entity, as well as protected from the business's actions and debts.

Although it can be confusing, the owners and managers of a business entity are merely *agents* of the entity, which means that they're acting on behalf of the business. This can be even more puzzling with small businesses because the managers may be the same as the owners—so it's important to keep a clear distinction between the two. For instance, when managers are acting "on behalf" of their entities, they must designate the capacity in which they are acting and maintain all of the corporate formalities; otherwise they may lose that corporate-veil protection.

We'll cover all of this in more detail in chapter 4 but, suffice it to say for now, the corporate veil does extend to other high-ranking members of your business, so long as you run your business properly.

3

How Your Corporate Veil is Compromised

E ven the courts will tell you that they are reluctant to pierce your corporate veil and will exercise caution in deciding whether or not to do so. Remember, the entire concept behind the corporate veil business structure is to encourage risk taking and personal enterprise. It was designed for our protection and benefit! So the fact that so many lawsuits against small business owners *still* result in the corporate veil's being pierced is more of an indication of how often small business owners fail to respect their corporate veils than the courts' eagerness to pierce them. In other words, if our corporate veil is pierced, it's likely nobody's fault but our own.

This chapter will detail the most common ways that small business owners compromise the protection of their corporate veil as well as highlight the specific reasons why courts will pierce them.

Operating in a Businesslike Manner

Although there are several factors that the courts consider when determining whether your business is legitimate and entitled to corporate-veil protection, ultimately what they're looking for is proof that your business is operating in a "businesslike manner." That means that your business is clearly separated from your personal affairs and strictly operates as a distinct entity from you, your partners, managers, and directors. It means that all formalities and legalities are closely followed and obeyed. And it means that your business pursuits and activities are for legal purposes and just intentions.

Essentially, operating in a businesslike manner means that you're respecting your corporate veil, as well as all related laws, with your business operating on one side, and your personal affairs clearly operating on the other. If you're operating in this manner, the courts should see no reason to pierce your corporate veil.

Primary Reasons Judges Pierce the Corporate Veil

If you do find your small business on the defensive end of a lawsuit, and you're accused of not operating in a businesslike manner, there are three main reasons why a court may agree and choose to pierce your corporate veil:

1. If they find that the business is your **alter ego**,
2. If **fraud was committed** by you through the business, and/or

3. If **justice requires it** because a creditor or other third party was harmed due to the business's failure to operate in a businesslike manner.

Alter Ego Theory

This is where small business owners, in particular, so often get themselves into trouble.

When courts pierce a corporate veil under the "alter ego theory," it's because they find a lack of separation between the owners and the business. If the owners fail to respect the corporate veil, a court may determine that the business entity is really just an alter ego of the owners; meaning that the owners are operating the business as if the formal business entity doesn't even exist. Courts will often interpret this to mean that the business is a sham (even if that wasn't the owner's intent) and pierce the corporate veil so that they can see what's really going on behind the scenes.

In order to avoid accusations that your business is merely an alter ego, it's extremely important that you observe all corporate formalities and make sure that the business entity is, in fact, a stand-alone and separate entity.

Small business owners, in general, are much *less likely* than large corporate owners to observe and respect the many corporate formalities, such as recording important decisions through meeting minutes or signing contracts "on behalf of the business" rather than as themselves. Sometimes it's because small business owners think that they don't have to be so formal, and sometimes it's simply because they don't understand what's expected of them. Either way, they're putting themselves at risk. Appreciate the fact that a small business owner who fails to follow corporate formalities is actually going to be *more* vulnerable to a piercing of the corporate veil. Courts will assume that your small business is just a façade designed to shield you from financial responsibility for debts and liabilities.

Aside from the operating formalities, special attention should also be given to the financial compliance of your business entity. This means that the entity must have:

- ✓ Adequate capital to operate and avoid undercapitalization,

- ✓ Separate books and bank accounts, and

- ✓ Proper records of the corporation or LLC's financial decisions.

These among other things, will provide proof to the courts that you weren't frivolously diverting funds, spending money, or obtaining credit simply for your own personal benefit.

In particular, commingling assets is always a big red flag that a business entity is just an alter ego. Commingling assets is when you use business dollars and accounts for personal expenses, and vice versa. Small business owners are much more likely to be guilty of this oversight. When you're the owner, manager, *and* financial officer of your business (the only person with access to the credit cards and general ledger!), it's far too easy to use that business credit card to buy a few personal groceries on the way home from work. While this may seem harmless to a small business owner, to the courts it's a very big deal.

Committing Fraud

Fraud, of course, is a surefire way to get any court's attention. While I won't spend time lecturing you on the ethics and morality of being a good person and running a business with pure motives, it's important to note here that sometimes an activity can appear to be fraudulent, even if that wasn't your intent; but the courts don't necessarily care. Making hasty or reckless business deals, for example, can sometimes appear to be fraudulent. Perhaps you agreed to a bad deal in the heat of the moment. If it was irresponsible or reckless, the court may rule that it was fraudulent activity. Similarly, accruing excessive debt can lead a court to believe that you deliberately borrowed money through the business, hoping to avoid paying it back in the future.

Another unfortunate, but all-too-common, example is when a small business is going bankrupt, so the owner creates another entity and transfers all of the assets to the new company, hoping that he can salvage his finances by avoiding having to pay off the struggling business's liabilities and debts. Even if the new entity is designed to be a legitimate business, this transfer of assets is still fraudulent and may give the courts enough reason to lift the corporate veil and strip the owner of his protection from personal liability.

The presence of a *shell entity* can also be cause for the courts to suspect that you're guilty of fraud. A shell

◊ segment

entity is a corporation that is established without any real business activity or property and resources. It's just kind of there, hoarding money. There are only a few legitimate reasons for opening a shell corporation, such as raising funds for a start-up. However, shell corporations rarely make sense for a small business owner.

If you do establish a shell corporation (for a lawful reason), be cautious how you use it. If you use the shell corporation (known as the parent corporation) to dominate the corporation or LLC that actually holds and owns your business activity (known as the subsidiary company), it's going to appear to the courts that your shell corporation is being used as a tax-avoidance shelter. For example, if your shell corporation (or you, as the controlling shareholder of the parent corporation) is heavily involved in the day-to-day operations of the subsidiary company such as making important policy and business decisions without consulting the subsidiary's directors or officers, or delivering guidance and instructions directly to the subsidiary's employees then you're jeopardizing the subsidiary company's independent status. In other words, if your subsidiary company is doing all the actual work but the parent company is holding the money and making decisions, the courts aren't going to like it. You've blurred the dividing line that is your corporate veil, and now they're going to pierce it.

Finally, enterprise entities can also be considered fraudulent and trigger the lifting of your corporate veil if not clearly maintained. An enterprise entity is when a single business venture is divided into different corporations. For example, if you own and operate several local daycare centers and the buildings are held by one corporation, the equipment is owned by another, and the buses or vans are owned by yet another, you have yourself a set of enterprise entities. This often seems suspicious to courts, which view the enterprise entities as a way for each corporation to minimize its assets and liabilities. Therefore, each entity needs to have its own set of books and records, and the agreements need to be made under fair-market conditions.

Fraud is a complex area of business ownership. Intent is not always the deciding factor, and the mere appearance of being fraudulent can be enough for you to lose your corporate-veil protection. This doesn't necessarily mean that you'll be found guilty, but the courts will want to scrutinize your records and business activity to find out for sure. While this should never scare you away from small business ownership, it is important that you follow all laws and corporate formalities, as well as make ethical decisions in all of your business dealings. The corporate veil was not designed to protect us from reckless or irresponsible behavior. Later chapters of this book will explain, in detail, how to stay in compliance and run your business legally so that fraud should never be an issue. However, if you're ever unsure whether your business activities or operations are fraudulent, our offices are here to help.

Justice Requires It

This one is pretty simple: If a creditor or litigant is left with an unpaid judgment or bills, because you operated your business fraudulently or as an alter ego, the courts may pierce your corporate veil simply because justice requires it. In other words, if a third party is harmed due to your lack of respect for your corporate veil and the laws, the courts will strip your corporate-veil protection so that the third party can be paid back and made whole again.

One important note here is on "derivative suits." A derivative suit is when shareholders of a corporation file a lawsuit on behalf of the corporation itself, usually against the directors, managers, or officers, for breaches of duty, mismanagement, or misappropriation of corporate assets. If the courts agree with the claims of the shareholders, they may pierce the corporate veil that protects every owner, manager, director, and officer in order to enforce a right, remedy a wrong, or return assets and funds to the corporation.

Shareholders have a tremendous number of hurdles to overcome in order to successfully bring a derivative suit, but they do happen and they are a risk to your corporate-veil protection.

Piercing the Corporate Veil: A Recap

Remember, your corporate veil is established for your protection! It allows you to take risks and chances in the uncertain world of business, without the fear of losing your personal assets. But this protection comes with responsibility. If you disrespect your corporate veil, commit fraud, or harm others, you'll lose your protection and face the consequences.

Courts will generally ask the following questions, among others, when deciding whether or not to pierce your corporate veil:

- ▶ Is the entity operating as a legitimate business?
- ▶ Is there commingling of business funds with personal funds?
- ▶ Are there clear records of the entity's business decisions and finances?
- ▶ Has the entity been set up for an abusive purpose?
- ▶ Are there assets in the entity or is it merely a shell?
- ▶ Does the business have adequate capital?
- ▶ Have others been harmed due to your business operations?

Now that you understand the risks of small business ownership and the ways you can jeopardize your corporate-veil protection, I'll walk you through the process of establishing your business structure, creating a solid entity, and running a compliant business operation.

4

Creating Your Business Entity in Five Main Steps

For some reason, our culture has placed an air of mystery around forming and filing a business entity. Far too many of us are intimidated by the prospect, believing that starting a business is either a rich-man's game or completely impossible without a specific degree or certain level of education. While I admit that the legalities are complex (which is why you're reading this book!), the idea that business formation is only for members of some secret club is simply not true, and it's high time we squashed that rumor.

The reality is that forming and filing a business is a process that can be broken down into five main steps, and is achievable by anybody who's willing to put in the work and think things through. Each type of entity requires different formalities, but here I'll give you an overview of the five basic steps. It will help you to see the bigger picture before we move on to the finer details.

Step #1—Naming Your Business

Once you've made the decision to go into business for yourself, you've got to decide what the business will be called. This may seem trivial in comparison to other matters, but it's actually a critical first step that will affect many other areas of your business formation.

From a legal perspective, it's important to decide on a name early on so that you can be sure that somebody else isn't already using it and secure the name for yourself. Nothing is more disappointing than spending time and money to create a business model that revolves around a particular name, just to find out later on that the name is already in use and, therefore, unavailable to you. Even worse is launching a business with a name that infringes on another business's trademark-protected name. This could lead to costly lawsuits, expensive rebranding, and wasted time.

From an operational perspective, your business name will represent your products, services, and everything your business stands for. It will be the face of your business and the first thing people see on your business cards. Marketing, name recognition, intellectual property, and a slew of other issues are all dependent on your choosing a fitting and available name for your new business venture.

Some of you will find the process of naming a business exciting, while others will see it as a tiresome challenge. Whatever your position on the matter, there are several factors to consider that will make the process easier and ensure that you choose just the right name for your business.

Naming Tips

First and foremost, it's important that the name does not create a likelihood of confusion as to whom the client is doing business with. Specifically, it's almost never advisable to use your personal name as your business name because it could blur that critical dividing line. Plaintiffs' attorneys could argue that their clients didn't know whether they were doing business with you, the individual, or you, the business entity. (This logic is somewhat different for medical professionals, however, so you may contact our offices to discuss the specifics of the medical field.)

For example, if your name is Bob Evans, it probably wouldn't be wise to name your new firework stand *Bob Evans' Big Boom Fireworks*. It leaves the door wide open for a plaintiffs' attorney to cry "confusion" as to whether a formal business entity actually existed. And this could lead to your being named personally as a defendant.

In choosing a name for your business, you could consider aligning it directly with the particular trade or industry that you're entering or the market that you're targeting. For example, if you're launching a line of eco-friendly lawn and garden tools, you may choose a name like Eco-Lawns or Greener Gardens.

Some find naming a business stressful, specifically because they want to come up with a name that conveys power or influence in their industry. In reality, that's not always essential to your success. Think of some of today's most profitable brand names. Many of them don't even mean anything! Amazon.com, for example, has nothing to do with the rain forest. Google is intentionally misspelled and, let's face it, kind of a silly word. And Etsy? Who even knows what that means? But, they work.

The goal and point here is to strike a balance; make sure the name isn't contradictory to your industry and marketing goals, but don't be afraid to think outside the box and get creative.

A few other things to consider:

▶ If you're not a licensed professional, then you should not use a name that implies that your business offers professional services. If you're selling vitamins and supplements, for example, but you're not a licensed medical professional, you probably shouldn't name your business *Vitamins, M.D.*

▶ If your business will be expanding into additional markets, make sure the name isn't so narrow that it pigeonholes your business into only one segment, geographical area, or trend.

▶ Make sure the name is not offensive to any culture or group. This will take some research, but it will save you and your company some embarrassment, and possibly even a lawsuit.

▶ Keep in mind that you will need a domain name for your business website and, therefore, the name should be spelled like it sounds. The last thing you want to do is lose potential business simply because a prospect couldn't find your website because the domain name doesn't fit or make sense.

▶ Once you've brainstormed and researched a couple of names, you may want to poll your friends and family to get their input. If at all possible, poll a few people in your target market and get their thoughts and opinions as well.

Important Name Searches

Before you set your heart on the perfect name, there are three searches you'll need to perform. These searches will guarantee that the name is available and that you're not infringing on another company's trademark rights.

▶ First, you'll need to visit the secretary of state website to make sure that the name is available in the state where you are filing. (We'll talk about state filing in steps 2 and 5!) Most sites have a feature where you can quickly check the availability of a name by performing a simple search.

▶ Next, you'll want to make sure that a domain name will be available. In other words, if the name Greener Gardens is available through the Secretary of State, but the domain name is already being used, then you may want to reconsider the name. The domain name doesn't necessarily need to be an exact match with your business name, but it does need to be very close and something that makes sense so that customers can easily find it.

▶ Finally, you'll want to check with the U.S. Patent and Trademark Office website and do a trademark search for the name you want. If the name is trademarked, and it's being used by a business similar to yours or in close geographical proximity, then it may be off limits.

Protecting Your Business Name

Finally, once you've chosen the name of your business, and cleared its availability, you will probably need to protect it by registering it with the U.S. Patent and Trademark Office. You may not need to worry about filing a trademark for your business if you're not planning on expanding or your market is in a small geographical area. However, if you do have plans to expand nationally, or even to more than one state or region, then you will need to file a trademark application for your business name. In fact, it's almost never a bad idea to do this anyway. Registering your business name as a trademark will offer your business added protection.

Step #2—Choosing the State of Incorporation

Once you've decided on a name for your business and cleared it through the three searches, you'll need to decide which state to file your entity in. (Remember, you'll want to check the secretary of state website for name availability before you decide on a final business name.)

At first glance, choosing your state of registration may seem like a no-brainer. Generally speaking, you'll want to file the business in the state where your business is located. If you're running a pizza shop in Denver,

Colorado, for example, then you'll want to file in Colorado. If your business does expand to other states, then you'll want to register the company in every state you expand to. Some professionals will tell you that it's a burden to file in every state where you have a business presence, but it's actually a benefit to your business because your business will gain specific protections under each state's statutes.

However, if you're launching a business that will immediately operate in multiple states, or that won't necessarily have a relationship with any one state in particular (like an online market), then you have the option of choosing a state that offers better tax- and asset-protection measures.

Many articles and books have been written on the benefits of incorporating a business in Delaware, Nevada, or Wyoming. Delaware's tax structure and shareholder protections make it a very popular state for registering publicly traded companies. On the other hand, Wyoming and Nevada offer advantages for holding and protecting assets such as brokerage accounts, savings accounts, and interests in other businesses. Both states have incorporated superior asset-protection laws into their statutes. Don't automatically assume that one of these three states will be better for your business, though. Do your research before deciding.

Step #3—Selecting the Tax Structure of Your Business

You can't avoid taxes, of course, but you can minimize them and make sure that you're not paying too much.

Choosing the right tax structure for your business, then, will be an important consideration. The type of business entity that you register as will determine how your business is taxed. So when you choose whether to register as a sole proprietor, partnership, C Corporation, S Corporation, or Limited Liability Company, you're essentially deciding how you want the IRS to identify your business and, therefore, how you want them to tax it.

There are advantages and disadvantages to each tax structure, and most are better suited for certain businesses over others. Chapters 5 through 7 will cover each tax structure in detail, but we'll briefly go over them here and highlight the main advantages and disadvantages of each.

Sole Proprietor

The simplest, most basic option for taxation is the sole proprietor. Under a sole proprietorship, you are the sole owner and would simply report the business's profits or losses on your personal tax return. Businesses that have little to no liability, don't sell products, and don't offer services with risk are usually better candidates for sole proprietorships than others. For example, if you offer part-time tutoring, local house cleaning, or freelance writing, you may consider being a sole proprietor.

► **Advantage**—You'll have complete control over your business and there will be very few legalities or forms to complete. It's a very straightforward form of taxation.

▶ **Disadvantage**—A sole proprietorship offers zero corporate-veil protection; no corporate veil and no dividing line. You and your business will literally be one in the same. That's why it's best suited for businesses with little to no risk and very small operations.

Partnership

If you'll own and finance the business with at least one other person, you'll have to choose between a partnership and a corporation. Partnerships are taxed just like sole proprietorships. The profits and losses flow through the business straight to the owners. Each partner will file Form 1065, and the profits or losses will be allocated to each partner on a K-1 form.

Much like a sole proprietorship, partnerships are best suited for small business ventures with little risk. For example, if you're financing a small bookkeeping firm or marketing agency that will only serve local businesses, then a partnership may be an affordable and suitable option for you. If business starts booming, and you add employees or branches, you can always adjust the tax structure and file as a corporation.

▶ **Advantage**—They're very simple to operate. There are very few formalities, other than signing a basic partnership agreement, and the profits flow directly to the owners.

► **Disadvantage**—Business owners in a partnership have no corporate-veil protection. Plus, not only are you responsible for your own professional actions, but you're also responsible for the professional actions of your partner. If you choose this tax structure, make sure that you choose your partners wisely.

C Corporation

The corporate tax structure, in general, offers many benefits that are not available to sole proprietorships and partnerships; most significantly, the corporate-veil protection. All corporations start off as C Corporations. A special form is required to adjust a C Corporation to an S Corporation, which we'll discuss in detail in just a moment.

The key to a C Corporation is that it's taxed separately from its shareholders (the owners). The C Corporation, itself, pays taxes on any profits left over after expenses. However, this often means that C Corporations are subject to *double taxation*. Double taxation is a result of the corporation's paying taxes at the corporate level and then the shareholders' paying taxes on the money that is distributed to them from the corporation. Even so, C Corporations can be very useful when the shareholders want to keep cash in the corporation to pay for equipment, pay down debt, or further the growth of the company. Another benefit of the C Corporation is that a C Corporation has its own tax rate.

► **Advantage**—The clear advantage of a C Corporation is the corporate-veil protection it offers. Every shareholder, director, and officer will have his personal assets shielded from liability and clearly separated from the business's activities.

► **Disadvantage**—Double-taxation can be costly and isn't always the best choice, depending on how your company operates.

S Corporation

The S Corporation is classified as a pass-through entity, which means that the entity itself is not subject to taxation. The profits and losses pass through to the shareholders' tax returns just as they do with the sole proprietorship, and thus avoid the double taxation of a C Corporation. But it offers the same liability protection for the shareholders as a C Corporation, so long as they respect the corporate veil. One benefit of an S Corporation is that the shareholders can draw "reasonable" salaries and still receive distributions. (We'll go over the difference in chapter 6.) The salary is taxed as earned income, which is subject to employment tax, while distributions are taxed at a lower rate than ordinary income. There are some disadvantages of an S Corporation, such as less flexibility in allocating profits and losses.

► **Advantage**—Owners and shareholders enjoy corporate-veil protection and pay fewer overall taxes than a C Corporation.

▶ **Disadvantage**—S Corporations are expensive to create and require a lot of paperwork and formalities to correctly maintain. Income is also allocated to owners according to their ownership interest, so there can be limitations to owner income.

Limited Liability Company (LLC)

As far as business entities are concerned, the LLC is the new kid on the block. It was first introduced by the Wyoming State Legislature in 1977 and has experienced a dramatic rise in popularity ever since. LLCs are popular because they combine the best of sole proprietorships with the best of corporations, and also offer a level of flexibility that you won't get out of any other tax structure. For example, LLC owners can choose whether to have the business taxed as a partnership or as a corporation. In other words, you can choose to have the business itself taxed, or choose to have the taxes flow directly to you. LLCs also offer their owners the benefits of corporate-veil protection. As good as this all sounds, LLCs aren't the right choice for every business entity. Compared to sole proprietorships and partnerships, LLCs are much more expensive to operate and have many more formalities.

▶ **Advantage**—LLCs offer many advantages, the main one being their flexibility. They're a good mix of partnership tax benefits and corporate liability protection.

► **Disadvantage**—LLCs are more complex to maintain than partnerships. In addition, state laws are still evolving on the use and maintenance of LLCs so they don't always reflect the latest federal tax changes. This can make it tricky to stay in compliance.

Chapters 5 through 7 discuss each different tax structure in more detail and explain their legalities and operating procedures.

Step #4—Choosing the Management Team

The fourth step in creating your business entity is to assemble the management team that will help lead and run your business. A sole proprietorship, of course, will consist of you and you alone. Partnerships are fairly simple as well. Typically, you have one or two partners, at most, and you finance a small business together, sharing equally in the profits and losses. Here, we'll focus on the corporation and LLC management teams.

Corporations

Corporations need shareholders, directors, and officers. The shareholders own the company's stock. In other words, the shareholders are generally the folks who contribute the funds, cash, and assets necessary to get the business off the ground. You may be the only shareholder or you may have a dozen others, depending entirely on how you choose to finance and launch your business. State laws can also dictate how many shareholders you can and are required to have, so be sure to check the laws in the state where you choose to register your business. The shareholders are then tasked with electing directors to carry out the broad policy of the corporation, and directors are responsible for hiring officers to carry out the mission. All states will allow you to hold all of these titles, but you still have to respect the formalities of each position.

LLCs

Limited liability companies differ somewhat in their management structure. The owners of an LLC are known as members. The members are responsible for selecting managers, and the managers then make the decisions regarding the direction and day-to-day operations of the LLC. All states now allow you to be a single-member LLC (meaning you're the only owner) and also hold the position of sole manager. Again, if you choose to hold both titles, you have to be careful to respect the formalities of each position; which, of course, will help protect your corporate veil.

The choosing of directors, officers, and managers will be covered in more detail in the following chapters. What's important to understand here is that electing your management team is a crucial step in the business formation process. If you're working with partners and other shareholders, and choose to elect others to serve as officers and managers, keep in mind that you are giving some control of your business over to other people. This isn't necessarily a bad thing, because your business can benefit from the knowledge and skill of others, but it can also leave you vulnerable and put your business at risk. Choose your partners and managers with care and read the next few chapters carefully.

Step #5—Drafting and Filing the Documents

Once you've completed steps 1 through 5, you're ready to draft and file the documents to officially form your business entity. There are a few simple components to this step.

State Filing

Each state requires initial forms, or documents, to be filed when forming your business entity, and the type of form you need will depend on which type of business you're forming. While the titles and specific layouts of the forms may differ from state to state, they generally require that you submit the same basic information:

- ▶ A list of the business's management or leadership team members,

- ▶ The owners of the organization,

- ▶ The registered agent for the business, and

- ▶ The business's location.

In most states, you can simply log on to the secretary of state website to download the forms or fill them out online. Many sites require you to set up an account with a login and password. Accounts are free to establish, and you should keep the log-in information for future use. You'll need it when it comes time to file annual documents or amendments for your business. (Those will be discussed in later chapters.)

The IRS

After filing with the state, the business needs to be registered with the IRS in order to receive an Employer Identification Number (EIN). The EIN for a business is just like a social security number for an individual. Applying for an EIN is a free and fairly straightforward process that is done through the irs.gov website or by downloading the form and faxing it in.

When you apply online, you'll receive an EIN immediately upon submission. If you fax the application form, it will take about a week for them to send a return fax with your new EIN. Sole proprietors are not required to apply for EINs because they'll pay the business taxes under their SSNs. However, sole proprietors may apply for EINs, if they prefer.

County and City Filings

Finally, at the county and city level, you'll also need to file the applicable business licenses. This will be different for each and every business, depending on where your business is located, what kind of industry it is, how many employees you have, and more. The best place to start is with the secretary of state website. Most states' sites include very organized information on how to find out which licenses you may need.

Creating Your Business Entity: A Recap

Keep in mind that this is simply an overview of the basic steps required to form and file a business entity. Certain tax structures require more formalities than others. As I've noted earlier, those formalities will be covered in detail in chapters 5 through 7. What I want you to understand here, though, is that forming a business is not only possible, but also much easier when you break it down into manageable, logical steps.

As you move forward to the next section of this book, you should be able to decide which tax structure is likely to work best for your new business. Sole proprietors and partnerships don't offer corporate-veil protection, of course, but they do have their place and are sometimes the right fit. After reading chapter 5, you should know whether either of those structures is right for you, or whether you need to form a corporation or LLC instead. Read the chapters on those structures carefully, as they fully explain the formalities required so that you can successfully complete these five important steps. Then you'll be well on your way to running a legitimate and fruitful small business.

5

Sole Proprietors and Partnerships

Sole proprietors and partnerships are uncomplicated, straightforward business structures that require very few formalities or paperwork to operate and form. As was noted in the previous chapter, they both do offer a few advantages, such as simplicity and more control over your business. However, because neither formation offers the protection of a corporate veil, I'll spend very little time discussing the details of each.

Sole Proprietors

The most minimal way to run a small business is in the form of a sole proprietorship. Sole proprietorships, as the name suggests, consist of one owner/operator and no employees. The business is just you and you are the business. Even though the business is really just an individual, it can still be given an official business name. Often a sole proprietor will use the notation "dba" for "doing business as." Let's say Mindy Jones is operating a small bookkeeping service for local small businesses. Her checks and business cards may say, "Mindy Jones dba MJ's Bookkeeping Services." MJ's Bookkeeping Services would require no formal filings; it would simply be the name that Mindy gave to her sole proprietor business.

The most significant disadvantage of the sole proprietorship is the total lack of corporate-veil protection; the individual is responsible for all of the debts and liabilities of the business, no questions asked. Another disadvantage of sole proprietorships is that investors are very reluctant to invest in a sole-proprietor model. So if you have any plans or hopes at all of enticing investors or convincing lenders to give you a loan, a sole-proprietor model is probably not the right fit for you.

Still, sole proprietorships are not without their benefits. If you're operating a very small, local business, a sole-proprietorship model has no formalities and will give you full and complete control over your business. It's very simple to operate. There are no formal filings at the state or federal level and, as far as the IRS is concerned, the business doesn't even exist. Additionally, the sole proprietor model is an affordable option if you're starting out on a shoestring budget.

Even though the business doesn't formally exist, the individual owner still has to file the profits or losses on her personal tax returns and pay self-employment taxes on any income made from the business. The owner should also pay estimated quarterly tax payments. While it's not a strict requirement, failure to pay estimated taxes throughout the year can result in interest and non-payment penalties, especially if you earn a sizeable income from the business. Locally, the sole proprietor will need to comply with any local and state licensing requirements, depending on the industry and location of the business.

According to the Tax Foundation, in 2014 there were 23 million sole proprietors in the United States, so it's obviously not without its merits. As has been noted previously, there are businesses that can successfully operate under this model. Virtual assistants, housecleaners, small-operation bookkeepers, computer repair services, and freelance writers are common examples of sole-proprietor industries.

Partnerships

When two or more people are engaged in the pursuit of a profit, it's called a partnership. A partnership can be created formally or informally. An informal partnership exists when two people hold themselves out as partners or engage in a joint moneymaking activity by contributing funds, skills, property, or time. If the partners are only working together for a short period of time, it's called a joint venture. If the joint venture continues, it becomes a partnership. Similar to a sole proprietorship, the lack of formal formation doesn't mean that the business venture can't be given a name, and the partnership will still need to comply with all state and local licensing requirements.

A formal partnership is formed when a partnership agreement is drafted, agreed to, and signed by the partners. The agreement should outline how decisions will be made, how authority will be allocated and controlled, how the profits or losses will be distributed, and, most importantly, how conflicts will be resolved. If you're going to establish a joint venture or partnership, we don't ever suggest doing so without having a partnership agreement in place.

The biggest disadvantage to general partnerships is that the partners are held jointly and severally liable for the liabilities and debts of the partnership. That means that each partner can be held liable not only for his own actions, but he may also be held liable for the actions of the other partners. Usually, the partner with the deepest pockets is the one who has to pay the most. This disadvantage is a significant factor and should be considered strongly before you decide to form a partnership with anybody. The potential conflicts and liabilities often aren't worth the risks involved.

As with any form of business, though, there are also some advantages to partnerships. One benefit, as has been noted, is that partnerships are easy to form. In regard to their advantage over sole proprietorships, partnerships offer the benefit of having more resources available to the business. Each partner should bring something unique to the partnership, such as capital, a specific skill set, certifications, or knowledge. Sometimes two is better than one and, if you have the right partner, you can be a success with this type of business structure.

From a tax perspective, a partnership is a pass-through entity, just like a sole proprietorship, but only slightly more complicated. Partners must file Form 1065 with the IRS. Form 1065 is a tax return that reports the profits, losses, and deductions of the partnership activity. Form 1065 also shows the amount of income or loss being passed through to each partner through a Schedule

K-1, which is a simple document attached to the 1065. The partners then report their share of the profits or losses on their respective returns. The partners each pay income taxes and a portion of any employment taxes on the income they receive directly from the business.

One thing to note here is that each partner pays taxes on the *income* that is allocated, not how much *cash* is distributed. This is known as phantom income. Unfortunately, it's often a bad thing. Your balance sheet (which we'll go over in chapter 11) may show that there was a profit and, therefore, you technically received "income," but that doesn't always mean that you actually get any cash or payment out of it, especially if you're putting money right back into the business. For our purposes here, I won't go into further detail, but beware of phantom income if you operate as a partnership.

6

Corporate Structure and Formation

When most people think of business in the United States, they usually conjure up images of giant corporations with dozens of suited businessmen and businesswomen sitting around fancy, oversized conference room tables. I suppose, in some regard, this isn't too far off.

The truth, though, is that a corporation can just as easily be a small business, owned and operated by a handful of people. In fact, the corporate structure offers small business owners the corporate-veil protection they need while giving them the flexibility to grow, which makes it the ideal choice for many entrepreneurs.

The Cost of Corporate-Veil Protection

Every good thing comes with a price.

While corporations offer the invaluable protection of a corporate veil, they also come with a whole other level of complexity and a certain amount of responsibility. The added level of security offered by a corporation is only possible because there are formalities and rules to follow. The formalities and rules keep order and ensure that you're operating a fair and legitimate business. In return, you're given legal protection from the acts of the corporation. If you follow the rules, you get to keep your corporate-veil protection. It's that simple.

If you're inexperienced with corporations or new to business altogether, though, the formalities of forming a corporation can seem daunting and intimidating, with all the key players, laws, and moving parts. It's a lot to figure out.

Here, we're going to separate all those parts and rules, and discuss them one by one. Then you can see how they all work together to protect your corporate veil from day one. We'll go over the specific forms required to create your corporation; the different roles of your shareholders, directors, and officers; and the rules and regulations that your management team needs to establish at the birth of the business.

From there, forming a corporate entity should make a whole lot more sense.

State Laws

Historically, a particular country authorized corporations. Today, each individual state grants the authority for a corporation to exist within its borders. At one time, that meant that each state's corporate laws were completely distinct, and often they varied widely. For years, this caused problems and confusion among business owners who wished to do interstate business. Thankfully, in 1984, the American Bar Association created the Model Business Corporation Act to help promote uniformity among the states' corporate laws. As of today, more than half of all states have used this act as a model to create their own current corporate statutes and regulations. This means that the laws are more standardized across the country. It's important to understand, however, that while the basic structure of the laws is now mostly the same, some states still offer more corporate protections and benefits than others, and a few don't follow the model act at all.

The various state laws are key factors as you determine which state you should form your business in. For many business owners, the state that your business resides in will be the state you should file in. For others, a different state may provide more fitting protection. Remember, you can only choose a different state if you're doing interstate or online business; otherwise you *have* to file in the state where your business is actually located.

Forming the Entity—The Articles of Incorporation

When forming a corporation, the first document you need to file is called the "Articles of Incorporation." Without this form, your entity doesn't legally exist. As was noted previously, the form can usually be downloaded or completed online from the secretary of state's website.

The articles of incorporation will vary slightly from state to state, but they're usually somewhat self-explanatory, so I won't go into too much detail. In general, the articles of incorporation will ask for the following information:

1. **The unique name of the corporation.** Before completing the articles of incorporation, remember to perform your name searches. Your articles may be rejected if your chosen name is already in use. You may want to refer back to the information on choosing a name in chapter 4 to avoid having the name of your business rejected.

2. **The corporation's purpose.** Not all states require you to describe the corporation's purpose. For those states that do, most allow you to use what's called a "purpose clause," which is basically a generic or broad description of the purpose of your business. For example, you might say, "The purpose of the corporation is to engage in any lawful act or activity for which a corporation may be organized under the laws of this state." For those states that do require a more distinctive purpose, be accurate in your description, but not too narrow. If your purpose description is too constrained and you decide to expand your business later on, this purpose may end up causing problems for you.

3. **A description of the stocks.** This is where you have to specify the class of stock being issued, the number of shares you have the authority to issue, and, in many states, the value of the stock. This will be discussed in more detail shortly.

4. **The name of the incorporator.** This is the name

of the person preparing the articles. If you're completing the form on your own, you'll list yourself as the incorporator. If you hire an attorney who completes the articles for you, he'll list himself as the incorporator. This doesn't give him any control or ownership of your company; it simply notifies the state who completed the form.

5. **The name of the registered agent.** This is the company or person responsible for receiving service of legal process. In other words, there has to be a place designated to receive complaints and summons if your corporation is ever listed as a defendant in a lawsuit. Usually, the agent is an attorney or a corporate service company.

6. **The registered address.** The registered address is usually the main headquarters of your business. This is where your corporation will receive communications from the state, as well as legal process documents.

Once the articles of incorporation are filed and approved by the secretary of state, your corporation officially comes into existence and your corporate-veil protection is formally established. Now, you'll need to protect it.

The Key to Organization—The Corporate Binder

Throughout this chapter, you'll see me refer to the corporate binder. A corporate binder is the key to your organization and an absolute necessity. This binder will house everything from your formation paperwork and licenses to every set of meeting minutes you ever take. If your corporation is ever audited or involved in a lawsuit, your corporate binder will be one of the first things you're required to surrender for inspection.

Your corporate seal is an embosser, or stamp, which includes your corporation's official name, its year of incorporation, and state of formation. Historically, every time an important decision was made, the minutes, document, or contract that resulted was to be stamped with your corporate seal to show that it was an official decision. Nowadays, the seal is no longer a requirement in regard to corporate formalities.

Setting Boundaries—The Organizational Meeting

After the articles of incorporation are filed, the corporation is technically in existence and capable of conducting business. However, your corporation won't get very far in its corporate dealings unless you formally organize its operations by holding a preliminary meeting. This meeting is referred to as the "organizational meeting," and it's where you and your investors get to establish some rules and guidelines for the business and its operations.

At the meeting, you and your investors will decide how decisions will be made going forward, what record keeping and documentation should be maintained, how meetings will be run, the rights of the shareholders, who the management team will be, and so forth. Most of the decisions made will be recorded and solidified in the corporation's bylaws, which will be officially adopted at the organizational meeting.

We'll discuss all of this in more detail throughout this chapter. Suffice it to say for now, the organizational meeting is a critical foundational step and should not be overlooked. A lot of your corporate-veil protections will be fortified at this meeting, and the meeting itself provides further proof that you're forming a legitimate business.

The Management Team and the Corporation Hierarchy

The management structure of a corporation can be represented with a simple pyramid. At the base, or foundation of the pyramid, are the shareholders. The shareholders own and control the corporation by providing the initial capital. The shareholders then elect the directors, who occupy the second level of the pyramid. The directors are in charge of making broad policy for the corporation. The directors then communicate the desired direction of the company to the next level of management, the officers. The officers are in charge of carrying out the policies and the day-to-day activities of the corporation. We'll discuss each in more detail next.

Shareholders and Stocks

If you've never been involved in a corporation, the concept of stocks and shareholders may be unclear.

Shareholders are the owners of a corporation. If you imagine that your corporation is a giant pizza, you'll cut it into slices, and each slice will be known as a share, or stock. The shares can then be sold and the buyers become your shareholders. Their cash can help pump capital into your business and, in return, they get to share in some of the profits later on.

Most small businesses have ten or fewer shareholders, and many of them will be friends, family members, or colleagues. In many states, you can actually be the only shareholder. We'll discuss that in more detail later on.

Anybody who has invested in your business prior to the organizational meeting should be present at the meeting. These are your initial shareholders and, as such, they have the right to help make decisions from the beginning.

Class and Amount of Stock

Early on, you'll need to make two key decisions about your stock: how many and what kind. The total number of shares that a corporation can issue, or sell, is called the *authorized stock*. This is the number of slices that you cut your corporation into. Stock that is actually distributed, or sold, is called *issued stock*. You can have 1,000 shares of authorized stock and only issue 900 shares at the beginning. If your corporation needs to bring in more capital later on, you can sell some of the authorized stock that's still available or issue more authorized stock; which means that you would cut your pizza up into even more slices. Keep in mind that the more slices you cut, the smaller they are. If you do this, attention must be given to the bylaws in order to preserve the current shareholders' rights. Recall that the number of authorized shares has to be listed in your articles of incorporation, so you'll actually need to make this decision before the organizational meeting. It's not set in stone, though, and can always be adjusted.

For small business owners, it's usually recommended that you authorize no more than 10,000 shares and no less than 1,000, based on how many shareholders you want to have. You want the shares to be small enough that an investor who purchases just a few shares of stock doesn't end up owning a huge chunk of your business. As a small business owner, you also want to keep things fairly simple. Your small corporation probably doesn't need 10 million stocks and hundreds of owners like a large, multinational corporation.

Stocks are also broken up into different classes. Generally, those classes are *common stock* and *preferred stock*. By law, S Corporations may only have one class of stock while C Corporations can have more than one. The class of stock will be decided upon at the organizational meeting and will become part of your bylaws. Generally, smaller corporations will only issue common stock. Common stock includes the right to vote as a shareholder. Larger corporations will also issue preferred stock. Preferred shares include the right to receive dividends and other benefits not granted with common shares.

Shareholders' Rights

Ownership of shares in a corporation comes with key inherent rights: the right to vote for directors, change the bylaws, and make critical changes to the corporation's course of business. Keep in mind that a shareholder's control of the corporation is mostly limited to voting rights, and the number of votes each shareholder gets is equal to the amount of shares he owns. If you want to maintain overall control of *your* business, then make sure you retain ownership of at least 51 percent of the total shares. This will ensure that you always have the majority vote.

You may find that some of your shareholders feel as if they don't have much control over the business they invested in, especially if they're new at this. Be sure that they understand that ownership is just that, and it's not the same as management. (Perhaps you can give them a copy of this book!)

Shareholders also have the right to inspect the books and records that relate to the shareholders' financial interest. In other words, shareholders can't make day-to-day decisions for the business, but they can vote to force the directors to make significant changes. In order to know if changes are needed, they have to look at the records and books. For example, if your shareholders review your ledgers and feel that the management is doing a poor job of purchasing and budgeting, the shareholders can vote to force the directors to make changes to the purchasing and budgeting procedures.

At the end of the day, your shareholders have a legitimate interest in your business because they invested their own money in it and own a piece of the pie. When the corporation makes money, they make money. And when it loses money, so do they. So, while they can't affect day-to-day operations, they can vote for changes that directly affect the corporation's bottom line.

Directors and Officers

At the organizational meeting, you and your investors will vote to elect the Board of Directors, including how many directors there should be, and what their specific duties and limitations will be. All of this will be included in your bylaws.

Recall that when you complete your articles of incorporation, you will need to include an incorporator. If the incorporator is an attorney, she'll also be known as the nominee director, only for the purpose of having the authority to officially form the corporation. Once the articles of incorporation are filed, the nominee director/incorporator will usually "resign" prior to the organizational meeting and appoint you as the presiding director, unless you specify that you want her to appoint someone else; perhaps one of your shareholders.

The presiding director will have the authority to commence and run the organizational meeting. Then, during the meeting, you and your shareholders will proceed to nominate and appoint official directors. There are sanctioned forms for all of this, which can usually be found in your corporate binder.

When choosing the number of directors for your corporation, "the more, the merrier" doesn't really apply. The board will have to make countless important decisions over the course of the corporation's lifetime. The more directors you have offering input and opinions, the harder it's going to be to find a consensus on things that really matter. Although a simple majority is usually all that's required, you still don't want to have an overly large board constantly at odds with each other. Most states require that you have at least one director. Absent some restriction in the bylaws or articles, the maximum number of directors is unlimited. Just be careful what you do with this freedom. Don't feel that you need to find an army to fill all of these director roles. Most of your directors will just be shareholders who were also nominated to serve as directors.

Role of Directors

Whereas the shareholders merely have voting rights, the board of directors is basically tasked with managing the business's most important affairs and maintaining the direction of the corporation. If your corporation were a ship, the directors would be at the helm, steering your business along. Their job includes most legal, tax, and financial decisions, as well as hiring and setting forth the compensation for the officers.

This isn't an all-encompassing list, but your board of directors will typically make decisions regarding the following:

- ► Appointing corporate officers,

- ► Setting salary amounts for officers and higher-level employees,

- ► Establishing benefits,

- ► Authorizing the issuance of shares of stock,

- ► Purchasing insurance,

- ▶ Declaring dividends,

- ▶ Adopting a retirement plan,

- ▶ Approving the hiring of CPAs and attorneys,

- ▶ Reviewing and amending budgets,

- ▶ Amending the articles of incorporation or bylaws, and

- ▶ Approving the terms of loans to or from shareholders, directors, officers, banks, or other individuals and lending groups.

The board may have the authority to delegate certain decisions to the corporation's officers or special committees, but they should always reserve the right to approve important legal, tax, and financial matters, or any critical issues affecting the general management of the business. Keep this in mind as you establish boundaries for the directors at your organizational meeting. Make sure that they maintain control over the most important decisions, but don't be afraid to give them authority to delegate when it makes sense to do so.

Duties of Loyalty and Care

As you and your other shareholders choose your first set of directors, it's important to understand that your directors have a duty of loyalty to the corporation, so choose folks you can trust. This is true of the board, as a whole, as well as the individual directors themselves. When making financial and business decisions for the company, the directors need to take care that they are always putting the corporation's financial and legal interests above their own, and they should never use their positions for personal, financial, or other advantage. Just like you, they have a price to pay for their own liability protection.

For example, as a general rule, any business opportunity that comes to a director personally must be presented to the corporation if the opportunity is in the same line of business that the corporation is engaged in. Let's say that your corporation manufactures and sells golf clubs and golf equipment. One of your directors personally comes across an opportunity to buy a competitor's golf equipment inventory, because they're going out of business. That director would be obligated and legally bound to present your board of directors with the opportunity to buy the inventory before he could consider buying it himself.

If the director failed to present the opportunity to the rest of your board, and took the opportunity for himself, the director could be charged with self-dealing, which comes with personal liability, as well as permanent removal from the board.

While there are other specific ways in which a director can violate his duty of loyalty, the general idea is that directors have to put the corporation's financial interests above their own in order to remain loyal.

Directors also have a duty of care to the corporation. This means that they have to perform their duties with the same degree of diligence, care, and skill that the ordinary, sensible person would be expected to exercise under similar circumstances.

In other words, directors are supposed to be competent, rational, and logical, and are expected to base decisions on research and factual information. Decisions made on this basis are considered good-faith decisions and will be protected by what is known as the "business judgment rule." In other words, the business judgment rule protects members of your management team so long as they use common sense and morality when making decisions for the business. This rule applies even if a good-faith decision results in losses for the company, so long as the directors weren't breaching their duties to the corporation, committing fraud, or breaking the law.

Failure of the board of directors to function with due care, however, will constitute mismanagement, allowing for the removal of directors and possibly even compelling court intervention in your corporation. Directors who fail to act with due care are directly liable to the corporation for any losses the corporation sustains as a result of the directors bad-faith decisions. In other words, their personal corporate-veil protection can be pierced and they can be held liable for the company's losses, even if the directors didn't actually benefit from their poor conduct. It's also important to note that the board of directors isn't necessarily punished, removed, or held liable as a whole. If it's clear that only certain directors were guilty of mismanagement or fraud, then the innocent directors won't be held liable and may keep their positions on the board. In order to protect themselves, it's essential that meeting minutes be accurately kept. If a director clearly dissents to a decision or vote, she should make sure that her dissent, and reasoning, is noted in the minutes. (We'll discuss that further in chapter 10.)

The point, here, is that your board of directors will be afforded corporate-veil protection. But, just like you, they'll have to be responsible in their business dealings so that they can keep that protection intact.

Role of Officers

Officers represent the final layer of the upper-management pyramid. Traditionally, the officers of a corporation are the president, vice president, secretary, and treasurer, although a corporation can have more or fewer, depending on what you and your shareholders decide, and what your state's laws dictate. Recall, from earlier, that the officers are in charge of the day-to-day operations of the corporation and ensuring that the overall direction that's determined by the shareholders and board is properly carried out.

Here, I'll provide a brief overview of the role of each position:

1. **President**—The president presides over the corporation's daily affairs, delegates to the other officers, and executes the broad policy decided upon by the board of directors.

2. **Vice President**—The vice president is often "the mouth" of the president. He or she oversees the operations of the corporation and provides communication between the president and the lower management and other officers. The VP can also fill in for the president when the president is

absent or unable to act. In very large corporations, there may be more than one VP, one for each division of the company. This is rarely necessary for a small business, however.

3. **Secretary**—The secretary is the record keeper. He ensures that notice requirements are met for corporate meetings, maintains the meeting minutes, and ensures, in general, that record-keeping formalities are followed. Choose your secretary wisely because his record-keeping ability is critical to your corporate-veil protection.

4. **Treasurer**—Finally, the treasurer maintains the financial records of the corporation. Again, this is a critical position to your corporate veil. We'll discuss finances in more detail later, but financial record keeping can make or break a corporation, so ensure that your treasurer is competent and reliable.

Officers as Agents

Because your officers will be in charge of the day-to-day operations of the corporation, they'll often be the ones representing the business in public and in business dealings. In other words, they'll have the duty and authority to act "on behalf" of the corporation. This makes them agents of the business.

Your president, for example, may sign a lease contract for a major piece of equipment. In this case, the president isn't signing for himself. He's signing "on behalf of," or as an agent of, the corporation and, therefore, is binding the corporation to the lease.

When acting as agents of the corporation, your officers are held to the same level of loyalty and duty of care as the directors. This means that your officers have to base their decisions on facts and all available information, and that decisions made for the corporation need to be logical and made with due care. Officers will be afforded corporate-veil protection, recall, so long as they are responsible in their roles as agents of the corporation.

More on the duties of the management team will be discussed later in regard to the business's continued operation and compliance.

Choosing a Corporate Tax Structure

Let's talk taxes for just a moment; everybody's favorite subject, right? Okay, maybe not a favorite, but it will be one of the most important decisions that you and your shareholders make, so I encourage you to have a basic understanding of corporate tax principals.

When you file your articles of incorporation with the state, you're declaring that your business entity will operate as a corporation. This is all the secretary of state is concerned with. The IRS, on the other hand, needs a bit more information so they know exactly how to tax the corporation. At your organizational meeting, you and your shareholders will need to decide whether to operate as a C Corp or an S Corp.

The main difference, if you recall, between a C Corp and an S Corp is that an S Corporation is a pass-through entity, which means that the shareholders will pay taxes on the corporation's profits. A C Corporation, on the other hand, will file and pay taxes on the profits at the corporate level, and the shareholders will pay taxes on the dividends or distributed shares they receive from the business. We discussed, earlier, that this makes C Corporations subject to double taxation. However, C Corporations are also given more tax deductions.

S Corporations, if you recall, are limited to only one type of stock, and shareholders are generally limited to only 100 shares. (Keep this in mind as you decide how much stock to authorize.) This, and the S Corporations' pass-through tax structure, often make them better suited for small businesses than C Corporations. For that reason, I'll focus more on the S Corporation tax structure here.

Every corporation automatically starts off as a C Corporation when it's filed with the IRS, but you and your shareholders may vote to file the corporation as an S Corporation instead. In order to form an S Corporation, you'll need to file Form 2553 with the IRS within seventy-five days after filing your articles of incorporation. (This is one of the many reasons why it's so important to hold your organizational meeting in a timely manner.)

If you and your shareholders do elect to file as an S Corporation, you'll need to decide on a reasonable salary for the shareholders. Any profits beyond their agreed upon salaries would then be taxed at year-end as passive income. This is one of the many benefits of an S Corporation over a sole proprietorship or partnership, because passive income is not subject to employment tax.

We'll discuss taxation in much more detail in chapter 13. What's important to understand right now is that choosing your corporate tax structure is a critical step in your organizational meeting and should be considered carefully.

The Law of the Corporate Land—Corporate Bylaws

Your corporation's bylaws will essentially be the final "contract" between your shareholders and the corporation, and will include every official decision made at the organizational meeting. Once the bylaws are officially adopted at the end of the meeting, the bylaws become the law of your corporate land and will govern the way you operate from that point on.

Keep in mind that your state of incorporation will have statutes regarding your bylaws. Usually, the state laws provide basic, minimal requirements for what should be included and what type of protections and structure you should arrange for your business. While these statutes should absolutely be obeyed, keep in mind that you shouldn't limit your corporation to them. In other words, just because state statute defines the minimum amount of protection and organization your corporation needs to have, this doesn't mean that you have to restrict yourself to the minimum. As you and your shareholders make decisions at your organizational meeting, be mindful to tailor your bylaws to the specific needs of your business.

Bylaw Hierarchy

If you look at the rules and regulations that govern your corporation, it's important to understand where the bylaws fall in the grand scheme of things.

State laws, of course, must be followed first and foremost. If your corporation is not following state law, then you're not in compliance. After state laws, your articles of incorporation dictate any further decisions made by your corporate management. If a decision made by the corporation violates any part of the articles of incorporation, then the articles will trump the decision and negate it. Following the articles are the bylaws. Therefore, the bylaws are important, but they must also answer to, and be consistent with, state laws and the articles. Finally, resolutions, or decisions made through votes at the shareholder or director meetings, must be consistent with the bylaws, articles, and state laws. If a resolution is in conflict with any of these governing bodies and documents, then the resolution is invalid.

This hierarchy of governing laws is another perfect example of why good record keeping is so important. It can be easy to forget details, especially as your business grows. So keeping an organized record of your articles, bylaws, and resolutions in your corporate binder is essential to the uniform operation of your corporation. Don't trip yourself up, or risk your corporate-veil protection, by keeping sloppy records of your corporation's official decisions.

Note that bylaws, while permanent, are not set in stone. As the needs of your business change, the bylaws may need to be amended.

Organizational Meeting Minutes

Preparing the organizational meeting minutes is one of the most critical steps toward protecting your newly created corporate veil. Whereas the bylaws are a culmination of the final decisions that are made at the meeting, the minutes are a detailed record of everything that's discussed and considered, including votes that don't pass, opinions expressed, and ideas that are brought up but set aside for future discussion. They'll serve as proof that you're following formalities and treating the corporation as a legitimate business entity, as well as provide a record of who said what and how final decisions were eventually made.

Here, I'll go over the typical format of an organization's meeting minutes and discuss what should be included.

1. **Date the meeting was held**. Note that the meeting must be held before the list of officers is submitted to the secretary of state.

2. **Name of the directors who were present**. The names of the directors will usually include you and the others who were present.

3. **Name of the appointed chairman**. You must appoint a chairman to conduct the organizational meeting. The chairman can be anyone present at the meeting. The chairman's responsibilities include running the meeting and keeping order.

4. **Name of appointed secretary.** You must also appoint a secretary to fill out the organizational meeting minutes. The secretary can be anyone

present at the meeting and doesn't necessarily have to be the person who is officially elected to serve as the corporation's secretary going forward.

5. **Date articles of incorporation were filed with secretary of state.** Self-explanatory, right?

6. **Name of the initial incorporator/director.** This may be a different person than the one listed on the articles of incorporation if a new director is chosen at the organizational meeting.

7. **Stockholder names and details.** This will include the names of the corporation's stockholders, the type of stock issued, the number of shares each shareholder received for his or her contribution, the property transferred by the shareholders to the corporation in return for the shares issued, and the voting rights attached to the shares.

8. **Names of nominated director(s).** The directors *nominated* by the shareholders will be listed here.

9. **Names of elected director(s).** After nominating a director, the shareholders will vote to officially elect him or her. The elected directors' names will be listed here. Some states require a minimum of three directors; others allow you to have as few as one. Check your state statutes.

10. **Names of nominated officers.** After the directors have been elected, they must select the corporation's first officers. Enter the *nominated* officers, here. The nominated officers, just like the nominated directors, aren't necessarily the officers

who end up being appointed. Remember that this is a record of everything that is discussed and considered at the meeting.

11. **Names of elected officers.** Again, these are the officers who are actually elected.

12. **Date on which corporation's tax year will begin.** For C Corporations, the tax year can be chosen as opposed to an S Corporation which follows the calendar.

13. **Date on which corporation's tax year will end.** If your corporation chooses tax year beginning on April 1, then your tax year will end on March 31.

14. **Address of corporation's business office.** Your corporation's business office isn't necessarily the corporation's place of business. Keep in mind that certain states require your corporate business office to be an address in the state of incorporation.

15. **Name of banking institution and address.** One of your shareholders' first decisions will be whom the corporation will bank with. This can either be a bank or a brokerage firm.

16. **Specimen stock certificate.** You'll find this in your corporate kit or binder, and how you fill it out sets an example for the corporation's formal stock.

Keep in mind that your organizational meeting minutes may include other entries if you and your board discuss other matters at the meeting. This, however, represents the typical issues discussed and can serve as a checklist so that no important formation subjects are missed.

The One-Man Show—Running a Single-Person Corporation

As of today's date, all states do have statutes allowing a corporation to be run by a single person. This means that you can play the role of shareholder, director, and officer, and serve in every single position possible. However, even if you're running a one-man or one-woman show, you still can't skip the formalities. Everything we've covered so far, from the organizational meeting to the bylaws to determining salaries and duties, still has to be followed. It may seem a little silly to hold an organizational meeting with yourself but, if you want to run a corporation, it has to be done; even if you're the only person present.

If you decide to operate as a single-person corporation, you need to check your state's statutes, first and foremost, to see if there are limitations or specific guidelines. Second, the way that you sign documents will be of great importance. For example, if you're signing a contract as the president of the corporation, you'll have to note that you're signing as the president. If you're signing an IRS document as the treasurer, you'll need to note that you're signing as the treasurer. If your corporation is ever audited or sued and every single document and contract is simply signed by "you" instead of "*you* the president," "*you* the director," or "*you* the secretary," then you may very well risk your corporate-veil protection. The IRS or courts will view your corporate formation as a front to accrue debts and run a dishonest business. (Chapter 9 will cover this in more detail.)

I don't say any of this to talk you out of running a corporation on your own. There are instances where this may actually be practical and make sense. However, I do encourage you to be a stickler about formalities if you choose to run your corporation this way. It will be too easy to skip steps or ignore procedures when it's just you running the show, but this could cause you problems later on.

If you're looking for corporate-veil protection, but you don't want to run your business with a team, you may also want to consider operating as a limited liability company, which we'll discuss in chapter 7.

What Have We Learned?

There's no doubt that corporations are complex, but forming one is much less complicated when you know what's actually supposed to happen.

The steps:

- ▶ Your corporation will begin by filing your articles of incorporation.

- ▶ Next, you'll need to hold your organizational meeting. Your organizational meeting will be held to create and establish your corporate bylaws.

- ▶ Your bylaws will determine how your corporation will operate.

The key players:

- ▶ Your investors are your co-owners, otherwise known as your shareholders. The shareholders elect the directors and officers.

- ▶ The directors steer the direction of the corporation and delegate to the officers.

- ▶ The officers are the day-to-day operators and carry out the vision set by the shareholders and directors.

- ▶ Most small business corporations have a handful of people who fill all of these roles.

7

LLC Structure and Formation

Limited liability companies (LLCs) are a hybrid business structure combining the corporate-veil protection of corporations with the management flexibility of a partnership or sole proprietorship. Because they blend the best of both worlds, they've very quickly become the most popular form of statutory business entity. In other words, of all the business entities that offer corporate-veil protection, the LLC is by far a fan favorite.

For small business owners, in particular, the LLC is enticing. Corporations, as we've learned, tend to have lengthy regulations and tedious compliance procedures. The LLC is usually easier to operate than a corporation, but more structured than a partnership—which makes it a good fit for many small business ventures. It's not, however, without its setbacks.

LLCs and Varying State Laws

After LLCs were first created by the Wyoming State Leg-islature, it only took ten years for the concept to catch on nationwide. By 1987, every state had adopted statutes for the creation of LLCs within their jurisdictions. Just like corporations, LLCs are created by, and subject to, state laws. And just like corporations, every state is different.

The Uniform Limited Liability Company Act (ULLCA) was drafted and released in 1996. The goal, as usual, was to encourage the states to create more consistent laws regarding the formation, operation, and rights of LLCs. The original act received very little attention or response, however. Even though it was revised in both 2006 and 2013, still only a handful of states have actually adopted or conformed to it. This means that LLC statutes across the states have several differences and inconsistencies—sometimes even extreme.

It's also important to understand that the concept of the LLC entity is still evolving and taking shape. That means that several issues have yet to be decided by the courts, and state legislatures are still responding to the LLC's rapid growth and widespread popularity. This, com-bined with the variations in state laws, is one of the few disadvantages to running an LLC—especially if you plan on doing interstate business.

Point being, if you operate an LLC in multiple juris-dictions, you'll have to keep a close eye on changes in the law and understand how each state wants you to form and operate your business.

For example, if you form your LLC in Florida, but plan on doing business in both Georgia and Alabama as well, your business operations in Florida may have to look very different from your operations in Georgia and Alabama. It's not impossible to adhere to the variations, but you do need to be aware of them so that you can adjust and stay in compliance.

Forming the LLC—The Articles of Organization

An LLC is legally formed exactly the same way a corporation is—by filing the articles of organization with the secretary of state.

The articles are nearly identical to those of a corporation and include the name of the LLC, the manager(s), the business address, and the registered agent. Of course, one key difference will be the lack of information about stocks, because LLCs don't issue stock. (We'll discuss LLC ownership technicalities in just a moment.)

Most states require the LLC to file an annual report verifying or updating the information in the articles. A word of caution: this is a significant drawback to operating an LLC. Some states charge costly annual filing fees, sometimes based on the number of members. Because the articles are so similar to those of a corporation, I won't go into any further detail about them here.

Employer Identification Number

Form SS-4, Request for Employer Identification Number, formally creates the LLC in the eyes of the IRS. It's the same form you would use to request an EIN for a corporation. The form will ask for specific information regarding the LLC, such as the legal name of the entity, the address of record, and the county and state where the LLC was formed. The IRS will also want to know who the responsible party will be. In other words, who will be responsible for receiving notices from the IRS on behalf of the business? Typically, this is an attorney or corporate service company. Again, very similar to the corporation, so it doesn't bear further repeating.

Ownership

Your LLC management team will consist of members and managers. The members are the owners and the managers oversee the business operations. Their relationship is a bit more relaxed than the strict hierarchy of a corporation.

There are two ways to set up an LLC: member-managed or manager-managed. Member-managed means that the members are also the managers, charged with handling the day-to-day operations. Manager-managed means that some or all of the members will be passive owners, and somebody else will actually manage the business operations. We'll discuss both in more detail in a moment.

Members and Units

Instead of stocks or shares, LLCs issue "units" to represent ownership of the business. Members of your LLC will receive units in proportion to their ownership. The pizza metaphor still applies. If your cousin, for example, wants to purchase 30 percent of your LLC, he'll purchase 30 percent of the available units—or 30 percent of the available pieces of pizza. The other way this works is that if your cousin provides 30 percent of the start-up capital, he'll own 30 percent of the business.

There is no set or ideal number of members for an LLC to have. The goal is to be realistic. If your operations will be small and your business will only be local, you probably don't need ten members. On the other hand, if your LLC will be expanding into six other states, then multiple members may be beneficial.

All states allow you to operate with only one member. This is known as a single-member LLC, or SMLLC. If you operate as an SMLLC, you'll still need to follow formalities in order to protect your corporate veil. Just as with a single-person corporation, you'll have to continue to hold "meetings," keep meeting minutes, and follow the financial and accounting rules that will be discussed in later chapters.

Member Rights and Responsibilities

Just like shareholders, members of an LLC have certain rights; some derive from statute and case law but most will come from your operating agreement (which will be discussed in just a moment).

The main right is the right to vote on issues that affect the business, particularly profits. Other member rights will depend on whether the LLC is member-managed or manager-managed. In other words, if you and your two other members also manage the business, then you'll all enjoy the rights of both members and managers.

Similarly, your responsibilities will differ depending on which type of LLC you're operating. If you're member-managed, then your responsibilities will increase. If you're manager-managed and you don't serve as a manager, then your responsibilities will be few.

Another variable point here is that your members' fiduciary duties will entirely depend on how the business is managed. For example, if you have two members who don't manage, then they may not have a fiduciary duty to the business, unless you write it into the operating agreement. In other words, the managers will always have duties of loyalty and care to the LLC, but the members will only have a fiduciary duty if they also manage the business or you specify so in the operating agreement. Otherwise, they simply enjoy their voting rights and profit shares and are not otherwise bound to the business. As you draft your operating agreement, you need to consider this carefully and decide if you want to create language that will give your non-managing members some duties of loyalty and care to your business.

A word of caution here: a member's personal financial problems can eventually come back to the LLC and create challenges for the other members. This is true even if your members are not bound to a duty of loyalty and care. Either way, they still need to keep in mind that they're legally attached to your LLC and that corporate-veil protection is not ironclad. What you do in your personal life can and does matter in your business life; particularly when it comes to finances. So a member's personal financial problems can affect the business. (More on that later.)

Some states require the organizer of an LLC to be at least eighteen years old, but there is no age restriction to owning membership units. Unlike S Corporations, there's also no state requirement that members must be United States citizens. *But* the IRS will not allow an LLC to elect to be taxed as an S Corporation if one of the members is a non-citizen.

Finally, in most states, professionals such as attorneys, engineers, and accountants must choose to operate as professional limited liability companies (PLLCs). In a PLLC, all members must be licensed professionals.

Managers

Choosing between member-managed and manager-managed depends entirely on how much responsibility and control the members want to have in the day-to-day and general operations of the business. If all of your members want to be fully engaged in the management of the business, then you'll opt to be member-managed. Member-managed is the default selection in most states and works well with SMLLCs or LLCs with only a handful of members. However, member-managed has the potential to cause conflicts if the LLC has too many members. Remember, it's hard to come to a consensus when there are too many people at the table.

Opting to run your LLC as member-managed will also limit your ability to bring in additional members without also giving them management responsibilities and rights. Let's say that you launch with one other member besides yourself, and you operate as a member-managed LLC at the beginning. Three years down the road, you bring in a third member in order to boost capital and expand your services.

That new member would automatically become a manager as well, so you would have to ensure that you and your original members are prepared to start sharing management responsibility with the new member. It's not always a smooth transition and is often easier said than done.

If, on the other hand, you and/or some of your initial members want to be passive owners, uninvolved in the daily operations, then manger-managed may be a better fit. This also works well for large LLCs or those with multiple members. Managers are usually just members who are elected and agree to serve as managers, much like a board of directors. You and your spouse, for example, may want to be members *and* managers, but you may have three colleagues who want to be members of the LLC but uninvolved in the operations. You can also choose to hire a third party, non-member, or other entity to manage the LLC. Since most states only list the manager(s) in the filing documents, your passive, non-management investors can even remain anonymous.

Manager Rights and Responsibilities

First, as was noted earlier, LLC managers have a fiduciary duty of loyalty and care to the business. The managers must take care to always put the LLC's interests above their own and never use their positions for personal, financial, or other advantage. Remember, the LLC does offer corporate-veil protection, which will generally protect the managers personally from lawsuits and liabilities. *But* they have to protect that corporate veil by making wise and judicious business choices in an ethical manner.

Other management responsibilities will depend entirely on what you and your other members decide. You get to choose what the manager(s) will do on a daily basis, what their job descriptions will look like, whom they'll report to, and so on. It's a very flexible situation with very few statutory requirements, which is one of the many benefits of operating an LLC. You get to decide exactly what your manager(s) will be doing.

Similarly, managers of an LLC don't necessarily hold traditional titles like the officers of a corporation do. There's no strict hierarchy of president, VP, secretary, etc. One of the other flexible benefits to operating as an LLC is that you have the option to choose your own management titles. (How fun is that, right?)

Here are some common choices:

▶ **Owner**—If you're operating as an SMLLC, then you may simply want to list yourself as the "Owner." This is a surefire way to make it clear to outsiders what your role is.

▶ **Managing Member**—If you have just a few members and one is serving as the manager, then this title is a good designation. It makes it clear that you're both owner and manager but insinuates that there are also other members involved.

▶ **Chief Executive Officer**—The CEO designation sounds very official and makes it clear that the CEO is in charge of the management responsibilities. This can be useful if you have more than one manager, so that outsiders know which manager is ultimately in charge.

▶ **Principal**—This title is often used in LLCs that provide a service, rather than a product.

▶ **Director**—Finally, director is a popular title for LLCs that provide technology or creative services. This can also be useful if you have more than one manager, with each being responsible for a particular branch or aspect of the business. For example, you may have a marketing director, human resources director, and technical director.

One thing to keep in mind as you're choosing a title is that the point of the title is to make it obvious to outsiders who has the authority to sign contracts and speak on behalf of the business. If you're working with potential new clients or manufacturers, they need to know who actually has the authority to make decisions. This will also be important when it comes to your corporate-veil protection. If the title is unclear or questionable, the courts may pierce your veil to ensure that the LLC is operating properly and that not just anybody was allowed to move money, sign contracts, or open new accounts.

Taxation

Another key advantage to the LLC structure is that LLCs can choose to be taxed as sole proprietorships, partnerships, S Corporations, or C Corporations. Most SMLLCs choose to be taxed as pass-through entities. This means that the profits and losses flow directly to the member's tax return. A downside to this is that the deductions are limited to that of the individual. In other words, the business entity won't be allowed to make deductions, only you will.

When there are two or more owners of the LLC, the LLC will need to be taxed as either a partnership or corporation. The same rules that apply to partnerships and corporations apply to LLCs that are taxed like partnerships or corporations. Of course, tax rules that apply specifically to shares of a corporation are disregarded in an LLC.

Operating Agreement

Whereas corporations operate based on their bylaws, LLCs operate based on their operating agreements, just as the name suggests. Once the articles of organization are filed, you and the other initial members of your LLC should draft, vote on, and sign an operating agreement. Once signed, the operating agreement is a binding contract that is enforceable by the members.

Interestingly enough, most states don't actually require that you have an operating agreement, even though it will be one of the first things the courts look for if your LLC is ever sued or audited. (Remember, LLC laws are still evolving so they haven't really caught up to the necessity of an operating agreement.) Despite what your state laws may dictate, an operating agreement is essential to protecting the LLC's veil.

Generic operating agreement templates are readily available online, but they rarely provide any real protection. In fact, more often than not, they severely weaken the protections afforded to an LLC. Because very few states actually require an operating agreement, far too many LLCs are formed without one, or with a weak one, and the overlooked importance of this document is only discovered through a lawsuit or audit—and by then it's too late.

I want you to avoid this mistake at all costs.

A properly drafted operating agreement outlines, as the title indicates, the operations of the company, including:

- ▶ The rights and responsibilities of the members,

- ▶ The rights and responsibilities of the managers,

- ▶ Provisions for meetings and voting,

- ▶ Guidelines for the allocation of profits and losses,

- ▶ Buyout provisions, and

- ▶ Specific rules for how the LLC will be managed.

One of the chief problems with boilerplate operating agreements is that they are not tailored to each individual business. Every LLC is different and requires a unique and personalized agreement. For example, you may be operating an SMLLC in the state of Idaho for the purpose of providing chiropractic services. Your neighbor, on the other hand, may operate a ten-member LLC for the purpose of selling sports equipment in Idaho, Oregon, Washington, and Montana. Your LLC's needs will be entirely different from your neighbor's, so your operating agreements should have very different provisions regarding issues such as voting and member responsibilities. But, if you both pull the same template from the same free website, at least one of you is likely to find yourself with an operating agreement that will leave your business vulnerable to grievances and your LLC veil at risk of being pierced. It's simply not worth the risk.

The other gamble with template operating agreements is that they're not adjusted to suit the individual state laws. A sound operating agreement in Colorado, for example, may not be suitable at all in New Jersey. The statutes of your registered state must be taken into consideration when drafting your agreement.

The Folly of Mandatory Distribution Clauses

Regardless of the purpose, location, and size of your LLC, a mandatory distribution clause is one provision that should never be included in your operating agreement.

Mandatory distribution clauses determine when profit distributions *must* be made, even without the members' vote or consent. This weakens the bargaining and settlement powers of your members, and automatically puts your corporate-veil protections at risk. I'll explain.

Let's say that a member of your LLC is experiencing personal financial problems. His credit card company sues him and the court finds in favor of the creditor. In this case, the credit card company may be able to receive the member's quarterly mandated profit distributions, instead of the member.

Unfortunately, most of the operating agreements that my team reviews are drafted with these mandatory distribution clauses—and, often, it's much too late by the time we're asked to review the agreements. The damage is done and the corporate veil is already being lifted.

What's the moral of the operating agreement story? Your operating agreement, like a corporation's bylaws, will be the law of the land should you choose to form an LLC. The operating agreement should be customized to suit the needs of your particular business and its owners, and should never include a mandatory distribution clause.

Charging Order Protections

Charging order protections are particularly important to an LLC's veil, so I'll cover them in detail here. A member in an LLC owns economic rights and management rights. These rights are not connected.

A charging order is a lien against an individual's economic interest in a partnership, limited partnership, or LLC that is given by the court. As with other liens, the holder of the lien is entitled to receive the benefit from the property being liened. In the case of a charging order, the lien holder is entitled to the LLC member's profit distributions, but does not obtain the rights of management or influence over the LLC. In essence, the charging order does not protect the debtor, but it does protect the LLC and its members against being forced to go into a partnership with a third party.

For example, if you were to fall behind on your personal credit card payments or medical bills, your creditor could seek a charging order from the courts after obtaining a judgment. If granted, any distributions from your LLC would be diverted to the creditor instead of you, until the debt was payed off. The business entity itself would be unaffected, as would the other members.

It wasn't always this way, though. In days past, when a creditor obtained a judgment against a debtor who owned a partnership interest, the creditor could satisfy the judgment by taking the interest of *any* partnership that the debtor had ownership in. After legally obtaining the partnership interest, the creditor could then sell the business assets in order to satisfy the judgment, even if the business had other owners. In other words, the debtor could seize anything owned by the partnership or LLC itself, rather than just the distributions or portion owned by the actual debtor. This obviously had a negative impact on the other partners or members involved. Realistically, the creditor could put the entire partnership out of business because of the personal debts of just one of its members.

In order to protect the other members from being so adversely affected by the struggling personal finances of one member, partnership laws evolved and the charging order was born. The Uniform Partnership Act (UPA) first adopted the use of a charging order, followed by the Revised Uniform Partnership Act (RUPA) and then the Uniform Limited Liability Company Act. All states have based at least part of their statutes on these acts. However, some states have made variations that have either strengthened or weakened the original language.

Per the norm, state laws vary in the remedies they offer to the holder of a charging order, i.e., the creditor. For example, some states allow the holder of a charging order the right to receive the debtor's distributions, or income, from the LLC, until the judgment is paid in full. In states, called sole-remedy states, where the sole remedy is to sit and wait for distributions, the holder of a charging order is not allowed to take over the partnership interests, demand distributions, or have a say in the affairs of the business. In other words, he may be entitled to your distribution share, but that doesn't necessarily mean that he's actually going to get anything. He can't force your LLC to make distributions.

Other states have allowed for a remedy known as "judicial foreclosure." This is when the holder of a charging order petitions the court for the right to foreclose on the charging order by demonstrating that the distributions from the LLC will not pay off the debt in a reasonable time.

One popular argument among asset protection promoters (they're on our side) is that creditors who are awarded charging orders should be responsible for the taxes on the distributions that should have been diverted to them, but were left inside the LLC. This opinion is based on Revenue Ruling 77-137, which itself was based on a very narrow set of circumstances and, therefore, does not apply across the board. The main factor is whether or not there was an actual assignment of the debtor's interest to the creditor or if the charging order is a lien against the distributions.

In most cases, members of an LLC are responsible for the taxes on the income that flows to them from the business entity, even if no cash is actually distributed to them. This is another form of phantom income, and it actually comes from an IRS ruling. So far, the ruling has been interpreted to mean that a member who is losing his income distributions from an LLC still has to pay the taxes on the distribution.

However, if a creditor is able to get a judicial foreclosure, then an argument could be made that the creditor should pay the taxes. Remember, in a judicial foreclosure, the creditor isn't just entitled to distributions, he's actually considered an owner of the member's interest and, therefore, has control of it. This, in theory, should make him responsible for the taxes on the disbursements.

Phew! Charging order protections are a complex legal concept, so don't be ashamed if you need to read through that section twice. The main point, though, is that your personal financial problems can have a negative effect on your LLC, as well as your other members. If you're being pursued for personal financial debts, your creditors may be able to seize control of your income from your LLC, or your overall ownership in the LLC. The same is true of your other members. So, despite the fact that an LLC offers corporate-veil protection, charging order protections and personal debts can present a challenge.

The Moral of the LLC Story

Okay, I know that was a lot of information thrown at you, so we'll do a quick recap.

The Steps:

Your LLC will begin by filing the articles of incorporation.

- ▶ You'll need to notify the IRS and request an EIN.
- ▶ Determine whether you're going to operate as a member-managed or manager-managed LLC.

▶ Meet with your members to draft and execute the operating agreement.

▶ Avoid the mandatory distribution clause!

The Key Players:

▶ Your members are your co-owners; the folks who bought units and/or contributed start-up capital.

▶ The managers will manage the day-to-day operations. This may be some or all of the members, or non-member, outside hires.

8

Planning, Coverage, and a Little Bit of Help

Running your small business, while keeping it in compliance, will require a plan, a brand, some coverage, and probably a little bit of help. In this chapter, we'll discuss how to effectively run your business with a business plan, employees, insurance, and intellectual property, all while maintaining your corporate-veil protection.

Business Plans

The Small Business Administration says that half of all small businesses in the U.S. fail within their first five years. Of those that hit the five-year mark, only a third make it to their ten-year anniversaries

Why such grim statistics? Well, it's definitely *not* for lack of customers, money, or even opportunities. One of the most common culprits is simply poor planning. That's why no small business should launch without a well-researched and finely-tuned business plan.

I know you're probably thinking that a business plan seems like more of a marketing and financial matter, but, believe me, having a well-thought-out plan is critical to compliance as well.

Before we dive in, let's be clear about the purpose of a business plan. Ultimately, the point of a business plan is to state the mission of your business then outline the steps needed to make it happen. It's like a road map to help you stay on course to your final destination. When it comes to the compliance issues that are necessary to running and growing a successful business, your business plan can help you manage those details and ensure that nothing critical is skipped or missed.

Future Growth

One of the most practical uses for a business plan is to help you aim toward future growth. Your business plan should include details about future goals for your business: expansion, adding to your product line, hiring employees, etc. In addition to the goals, your plan should also include details and reminders about what it will take to meet those goals, including the legalities. For example, if your goal is to eventually expand to a neighboring state, your plan should include the legal requirements needed to do business there, e.g., filing requirements, fees, deadlines, number of LLC members. Or, perhaps, your goal is to grow your small sole proprietorship into a statewide corporation. Your plan should list the filing requirements to register as a corporation so that you have specific financial and organizational milestones and objectives to aim for.

Point being, your business won't make it very far if you're not in compliance—and a business plan can help remind you which compliance matters need to be addressed and met in order for you to grow.

Deadlines and Timetables

Another practical use for a business plan is to help you meet compliance deadlines and other timeframes. Some of the most well-thought-out business plans include timelines and timetables. For example, your business plan may include a timeline for paying off debts to your initial lenders and creditors, which is essential to staying in compliance and keeping your business out of court. Your plan may also include a timetable for annual filings, intellectual property renewals, and more. If there's a deadline, timeframe, or cut-off date, then it probably relates to a compliance issue somehow. Putting it into your business plan can help you meet those critical deadlines and stay on track.

Management Team

As you grow, you'll likely add members to your management team, in the form of directors, officers, employees, and contractors. Your business plan can be used to communicate to them. The business plan, for example, can explain to new directors and officers the financial status of your business, future financial goals, branding requirements, scope of business, your target market, intellectual property protections and uses, and more. In other words, if your business plan is up-to-date and properly written, new members of your management team should be able to read the plan and have a firm grasp of what your business is all about, where it's going, and what it needs to do to get there. For managers and officers, in particular, this can help them do their jobs better, which includes keeping your business in compliance.

Additionally, your business plan can include specific job duties and descriptions for upper-level members of your management team. For example, your plan may describe the duties of the treasurer compared to the duties of the bookkeeper, and why your business has both. Or your plan may describe at what point you need to add a CEO to help manage the growing team of officers. Point being, the business plan can serve as a place to keep organized descriptions of duties and roles. When everybody knows exactly what his responsibilities are, important compliance issues are less likely to be missed.

Use It or Lose It

My final piece of advice for your business plan is to use it! Review it. Read it. Update it. Stick to it! Whatever you do, don't just let it sit there. I can't tell you how many small business owners have spent time and money to create a plan, and then shoved it into a file, never to be seen again. Your business plan can only be useful if it's something you actually refer to, read, and honor. You should review it at least once a year, or biannually if your business is growing or changing at a rapid pace.

Employees

Running a small business may also require the help of employees. I've met many small business owners who shied away from taking this step, mostly out of fear; fear of the liability involved or fear of losing control of their businesses. To be fair, these are valid concerns. Hiring employees is a very big step in the life of a small business owner. But there's a way to do it with liability and your corporate veil in mind.

Employer Liability

Before we go into details, let's briefly discuss the concept of employer liability; that is, the idea that employers are ultimately responsible for the acts of their employees. Technically, this is known as "*respondeat superior*," which is Latin for, "Let the superior answer." In plain English, it simply means that the employer is accountable for the actions of the employee. The rationale for this theory makes quite a bit of sense.

First, keep in mind that employers (i.e., small business owners) are responsible for directing the actions of their employees, so it makes sense that you would also be responsible for the results of those actions. Second, it's important to remember that you're only responsible for your employees' actions during the scope of their employment—that is, when they're on the job and doing something that you specifically asked or required of them.

As a small business owner, you get to benefit from the fruits of your employee's labor, in the form of sales, profits, and products. *But* this means that you must also share in the mistakes and poor choices made by your employees—at least the ones they make while they're on the clock. Therefore, when an employee does well and brings in a new client or develops a great new product, you get to share in and profit from that victory. When the same employee harasses a customer or gets into an accident in one of your work vehicles, you have to share in that as well.

Employees vs. Independent Contractors

Now let's discuss the difference between an employee and an independent contractor. When it comes to liability and your corporate-veil protection, there are some very big differences.

The most basic difference has to do with taxes. When you have employees, you'll have to take taxes out of their paychecks, both state and federal. You'll also have to withhold FICA taxes—Social Security and Medicare. For independent contractors, on the other hand, you'll simply pay them the agreed-upon rate and it will be their responsibility to pay their own taxes.

That's not all, though. To qualify as independent contractors, they have to have control of their own work, training, tools, supplies, and hours. For example, if you hire a plumber to replace the pipes in your new building and he sets his own hours, brings his own tools, and provides other laborers to help, then he'll likely be considered an independent contractor. If, on the other hand, you're a landlord and hire the same plumber to be available at your apartment complexes daily, and you provide him with tools, daily tasks, and specific hours to be worked, then he's probably considered an employee.

In regard to your corporate veil-protection, employees will leave you more exposed to liability issues than independent contractors will. Independent contractors are generally considered to be under their own control and direction, so it's less likely that you'll be held responsible for their actions. In fact, most independent contractors are required (or at least advised) to have their own insurance and other forms of coverage.

Let's say that you are a landlord and you hire that plumber for a one-time job, replacing all the pipes in your new apartment complex. The plumber is clearly an independent contractor as far as you're concerned, as he works for a local plumbing company, provides his own tools, and sets his own hours and rates. Several days after the job is complete, one of the new pipes ruptures, causing flooding to a number of units. Several of your tenants sue for damage to their furniture and other property. If the tenants hire a shotgun attorney, she's likely to try and list you and your business as defendants. But she'll have a much harder time proving you're at fault because the plumber was an independent and licensed contractor. So long as you reasonably relied on that plumbing company to do good work, the liability shouldn't fall on you.

There are exceptions to this, of course, but, generally speaking, an independent contractor is going to be liable for his own mistakes and actions, and your business and assets won't be at risk.

Employee Solutions

While independent contractors may keep liability issues more at bay, that's not to say that you should never hire employees. For one, it's simply not always feasible to hire independent contractors. You can't man an entire factory or assembly line with independent contractors, for example. And two, hiring employees can have its advantages. They're often more affordable and loyal, and you can add to their job descriptions any time you like. There's also something to be said for having control over their hours, training, and how they approach their work.

When, and if, you do hire employees, you'll want to do so cautiously, so as to protect yourself and your business. Here, I'll highlight a few important points when it comes to hiring:

- ▶ **Do your research**. Before you hire someone, do your research on his background, skills, education, and employment history, as well as his criminal record. This is especially important if the employee is going to be working around children or the general public, or have access to other people's property. If you do your due diligence and carefully screen your employees, you'll be taking an important step toward protecting yourself and your business.

- ▶ **Communicate**. Provide a clear job description, tasks to be completed, and expectations for your employees. This will make it very clear who is responsible for what, and help prevent errors and oversights. Performance evaluations are important, too. If your employees are mishandling tasks or projects, doing performance evaluations (and keeping records of them) can help clear things up and get them back on the right track. All of this can potentially help prevent costly mistakes and liability issues.

▸ **Get coverage.** We'll discuss insurance in detail in just a moment, but insurance is an absolute necessity for every small business owner, with or without employees. When you have employees, it becomes particularly important. When an employee makes a mistake or has an accident on your watch, you need to be prepared to take responsibility for the consequences.

Insurance

No matter how much we may try, the fact is that running a business doesn't always go as planned. A customer may trip and fall in your store. An employee may have an accident in your work vehicle. A product may not function as planned in the marketplace. These are the risks that we take as small business owners and entrepreneurs.

When things do go wrong, our goal should be two-fold: 1) to protect our business and personal assets, *and* 2) to right the wrong or correct the mistake. Drawing a clear line between yourself and your business can protect your personal assets. That's where the corporate veil comes in. In order to protect your business, though, it takes insurance. You want to have enough coverage to pay for any damages that may justifiably be owed and to right any wrong that may have resulted from the acts of an employee, yourself, or one of your products. Insurance coverage can also further persuade a shotgun plaintiff's attorney to leave your personal assets alone. If your insurance coverage is enough to cover the damages for her client, then she'll have less incentive to try and tear down your corporate veil and go after your personal assets.

The topic of insurance coverage options could fill an entire book, so I won't discuss every detail here. What I can do, though, is highlight some of the most effective ways to insure a small business so that you can discuss them with your attorney and insurance agent.

- ▶ **General Liability**—For almost any small business, this is a must-have policy. General liability insurance can provide coverage in the event that your business is found liable for damages, especially to a third party. General liability covers a range of incidents and accidents, but watch out for the exclusions.

- ▶ **Business Rider**—Business riders are great for home-based businesses or sole proprietors. A rider is simply an add-on to your homeowners, renters, or general liability policy. If the UPS guy, for example, delivers a business-related package to your front door and slips, your homeowners won't cover it—but a business rider would.

- ▶ **Commercial Auto**—If your business will include commercial or work vehicles, then commercial auto coverage is a must. This will help cover damage or accidents to work vehicles, or injuries caused in a company vehicle.

▶ **Workers' Compensation**—If you hire employees, the law will actually require that you carry workers' compensation coverage. If one of your employees is injured on the job, workers' compensation will help cover the costs.

▶ **Business Owner's Policy (BOP)**—A BOP is actually a kind of package that groups together multiple types of insurance for a small business owner. It might include property insurance, general liability, and business interruption insurance, just to name a few. Packages can be customized to meet your needs.

▶ **Professional Liability**—If you're operating your business as a licensed professional, this type of coverage is vital. As a licensed professional, or the owner of a business that manages professionals, you know that you're held to a higher standard. Therefore, mistakes, omissions, and errors can quickly lead to lawsuits. Professional liability coverage can help to pay for those mistakes so that your corporate veil remains intact and your business assets are protected.

▶ **Directors and Officers**—Finally, if you have a corporation or LLC, the corporate veil protects your directors and officers, *but* certain actions or errors can negate their corporate-veil protection, leaving them vulnerable to personal liability.

Directors and officers insurance can provide coverage for those unfortunate events, so that their personal assets can stay shielded.

Remember, if you form and run a legitimate small business, your corporate veil should protect your personal assets, and those of your upper-level managers, from frivolous lawsuits and debts. But life is unpredictable. Accidents happen. Mistakes are made. And people make errors in judgment. When these things happen, you may be held liable as the owner and director of your small business. In order to protect yourself, your business, and your employees, you have to have the proper insurance. So don't skip this critical step in protecting your small business.

Intellectual Property

Intellectual property is the subject of thousands of lawsuits each year. During your days as a small business owner, you may very well find yourself on one end or the other of an intellectual property-based lawsuit; either as the defendant in a lawsuit, being accused of infringing on someone else's property, or as the plaintiff, suing another business over the unauthorized use of yours.

Just like insurance, this topic could take up a book of its own. For our purposes here, though, I want to just briefly discuss how your intellectual property should be protected and why.

What Is It?

Intellectual property is simply the ownership of your business ideas and concepts: the products you invent, the taglines and logos you design and use, and the websites and marketing tools you use to share and represent your business. These things create your brand and the identity of your business—and they're often worth more than your products and services themselves.

KFC, for example, would be nothing without its coveted secret recipe. That recipe is a trade secret, a form of intellectual property, and is probably worth more than you and I combined. Without it, KFC would undoubtedly just be some small, local fast-food joint and never would have reached the heights it has today.

Nike is another good example. If you're shopping for basketball or running shoes and you see that famous "swoosh," you know you're looking at quality—and you're probably going to pay more for it, too. If anybody else were to put that swoosh logo on their products, it would devalue Nike's brand and they wouldn't be what they are today. So that recognizable little swoosh is trademark protected and closely guarded.

I know these are big examples, and only a few of many, but these corporations started out small, just like you and me. But they protected their intellectual property, consistently provided good quality, and exploded in popularity as a result.

Let's get down to specifics now. Intellectual property consists of the following:

► **Trademarks**—Trademarks are the words and symbols used to brand a business. They include logos, taglines, and sometimes even sounds. (Think of the three simple notes used by NBC.)

► **Copyrights**—Copyrights are the expression of ideas in fixed and tangible form. In plain English, that means if you think of a book idea in your head, it's just an idea. But if you type it up or write it down on paper, then it becomes protectable by copyright because you put it in "fixed form." Copyrights for small business owners often include things like blog posts, articles, ebooks, and marketing materials.

► **Patents**—Patents are unique inventions, processes, and methods. For example, if your small business uses a one-of-a-kind algorithm to predict good house-flipping markets, then you may be able to patent the algorithm. Or maybe you invented a lawnmower/weed-whacker hybrid that runs on solar power. You may be able to patent that so nobody else can market the same technology.

► **Trade Secrets**—Finally, we have trade secrets. Trade secrets are different from the others because they require no formal registration with a government entity. In fact, that would completely defeat the purpose. Trade secrets are just that: secrets. And they must be kept that way in order to be protected in a court of law. For example, if you're launching a yogurt shop using your own secret vegan frozen-yogurt recipe, then you'll want to keep that recipe under tight lock and key, otherwise somebody else can use it and there would be nothing you could do about it.

Protecting your intellectual property often requires some type of registration, either with the U.S. Patent and Trademark Office (USPTO) or the U.S. Copyright Office (except for those trade secrets). When you register your trademarks, patents, and copyrights, it notifies the public that your business is the rightful and legal owner of those ideas and brands. Your business, alone, is allowed to use those ideas and concepts, especially in the marketplace. Any unauthorized use of those ideas would be considered infringement and would give you standing to sue for damages.

Intellectual Property and Your Corporate Veil

What does any this have to do with my corporate veil? (I know you're asking.)

First, this is yet another opportunity for you to clearly separate yourself from your business. If your business uses a logo, a tagline, patents, or copyrights, the business should be listed as the owner of those ideas, not you, the individual. If your business ever finds itself in an infringement lawsuit, either as the plaintiff or the defendant, you want it to be very clear that the business owned the intellectual property, not you. This will help prove that your business is not just an alter ego and that you and your business are acting as two completely separate entities.

Second, if you properly register, renew, use, and protect your intellectual property rights, it will reduce the possibility of your business's ending up in court for an intellectual property-related matter in the first place. In other words, registering and managing your intellectual property is an important compliance issue. Not only can it keep you out of court, but it can also help to ensure that you can continue to use the products and ideas that represent your business and make you money.

9

Get it in Writing: The Small Business of Contracts

From the moment you launch your small business, every deal you make and every agreement you come to will need to be properly documented. This is where contracts come into play, and *every* small business owner should know the basics of contracts. Properly creating and signing a contract can make or break a business deal and mean the difference between a well-protected corporate veil and a full-on investigation into your personal financial affairs.

Get It in Writing!

The first lesson in contracts is very simple: get *everything* in writing! Yes, I really do mean everything. Whether you're leasing a building, hiring employees, working with a new manufacturer, or simply buying a new phone system, the details of your business agreements should always be captured in a proper legal contract. There are three noteworthy reasons for this hard and fast rule.

First, oral agreements are actually legal in many circumstances. This means that the law, in certain jurisdictions, recognizes verbal agreements as valid contracts. The problem is that it can be nearly impossible to objectively enforce a contract when the details exist only in the parties' memories. Let's say that you hire a graphic designer to design a logo for your start-up. You tell him what you're looking for, discuss some ideas, and agree upon an hourly rate. One month later, the graphic designer submits a logo that looks nothing like what you had imagined. Furthermore, you were expecting three separate designs to choose from, not just one. The designer sends you a bill and expects full payment within fifteen days. When you call to dispute the bill and work, you find that the graphic designer has a very different memory of what you asked for. Because your agreement and the details of your conversation were never memorialized in a written contract, neither of you has anything to refer back to, other than your own recollections of what was discussed. You will have to battle it out and see if you can come to some kind of understanding, because the courts can't help you enforce an agreement impartially if it was never written down.

The second reason to use written contracts is to ensure that everybody is on the exact same page. The way that contract negotiations usually work is that one party will draft a contract (either using a template or with the help of an attorney) and submit the proposed contract to the other party. The second party will read through it, make suggested edits and adjustments, and send it back to the first party. This goes on until both parties are completely satisfied with every detail of the agreement. This gives both parties the opportunity to think about all of the minor details that might have been overlooked if they had simply agreed to some basics over the phone and left it at that. Thorough and well-written contracts take time to think over and review.

Let's say that you're negotiating with a local manufacturer to begin production of your new clothing line for veterans, firefighters, and law enforcement officers. The CEO of the company has her attorney draft a contract and sends it over to you for review. Within the drafted contract, the attorney has included details about where the manufacturer is going to obtain the materials needed to produce your clothing; something that was never actually discussed over the phone but could make a huge difference in the overall quality of your products. You might have completely neglected this important detail had the manufacturer not thought to put the details in writing. This now gives you the opportunity to make sure that their materials are, indeed, exactly to your satisfaction— and that it becomes a contractual obligation on their part to keep it that way.

The third and final reason for putting your agreements in writing is—you guessed it—to protect your corporate veil. When you put your business agreements in writing, instead of just shaking hands like "the good ol' days," you're making it very clear that your *business entity* entered into an agreement, and not *you* as an individual. In other words, when a written contract clearly demonstrates that your business is in agreement with the landlord, creditor, third party, etc., then you're taking an absolutely critical step toward protecting yourself from personal liability should the contract be broken or lead to disputes in the future.

Family and Friends

Small business owners are particularly inclined to hire, work with, and partner with family members and close friends. While there is nothing wrong with this approach (in fact, it has many benefits), it's important to remember that written agreements with these folks are just as important, if not more so. Far too many small business owners are prone to taking a more relaxed approach when working with family and friends. But I have seen time and time again the devastation that this can cause, both financially and personally.

Communication with family and friends concerning business matters is no different than with anybody else. You're still apt to have different memories of a conversation or misunderstand a key point if the agreement is not put in writing. The real problem is that these disputes often become more heated and more personal because you have an emotional connection to the other party, rather than just a business relationship. A dispute over a verbal contract can destroy a friendship and tear a family apart. So, while it may feel a little awkward to approach your friend about signing a contract, it can also help protect your business, your personal assets, and your relationships.

Contracts 101: How They're Organized

Looking at a contract, especially if you're new to the business world, can be a little confusing. Between the pages of legalese and the scattered, broken paragraphs, it can be a challenge to take it all in, let alone make sense of it. Here, I want to give you a brief explanation of how a contract is organized so that you can make sense of your future business deals.

The Introductory Paragraph and Signature Blocks

Every contract begins with an introductory paragraph. This brief paragraph is used to name the parties and the official date of the agreement.

For example, if your small property management company contracts with a local social media marketing firm, the introductory paragraph might read something like this:

> *This agreement is dated 3 June 2020 and is between LMNOP PROPERTY MANAGEMENT, LLC, a Missouri Limited Liability Company, and YOUR ONLINE PRESENCE, INC., a Missouri Corporation.*

This simple paragraph is more important than you may think. First, the agreement date establishes the date that the contract is officially enforceable. As of this date, the terms of the agreement are established and in full force. You and the other party are both contractually obligated to hold up your end of the bargain at that point.

Second, the way that the parties are listed establishes who the legal parties actually are. If the parties are listed incorrectly, without their full and true legal names, then it can drastically affect who is actually liable. The names should be listed exactly as they are with the secretary of state.

The parties' signature blocks at the end of the contract should then match the introductory paragraph exactly. You may leave out the state of formation in order to shorten the block. Minor details, such as capitalization, periods, commas, and how the LLC or Inc. are used, can make all the difference in the world, especially if you're working with a company that has subsidiaries with substantially similar names. (More on that in a moment.)

Fictitious Names

If your business uses a fictitious name, such as a DBA, you'll have to be careful how you use it in a signature block and list it in the introductory paragraph. The fictitious or DBA name should never be used *in place of* your company's full legal name, the name you registered with the secretary of state. But if your company is known as something else in the marketplace, then that name will need to be listed as well.

For example, if your property management company uses a DBA, your introductory paragraph might read:

> *This agreement is dated 3 June 2020 and is between LMNOP PROPERTY MANAGEMENT, LLC, a Missouri Limited Liability Company doing business as New Frontier Realty, and YOUR ONLINE PRESENCE, INC., a Missouri corporation.*

Listing the DBA *and* the proper legal name makes it perfectly clear who is entering the contract, and will help to eliminate any questions of liability down the road. The moral of the story is to be as specific and legally accurate as possible about who the parties are.

The Correct Legal Entity

That said, it's not always easy to determine who the actual legal parties are—but it's vital to protecting everybody involved.

Many large corporations, for example, do business through multiple affiliate businesses. Real estate agents often work independently through a larger agency. And small business owners routinely do business using a DBA or fictitious name. If the full and correct legal entity is not listed on the contract, then the wrong person or entity could be held responsible for any debts and liabilities.

The easiest and most reliable way to find a business's correct legal name is to pull its records from the secretary of state in the state in which it was formed. Most states charge a small fee to perform this search online, although some are free and others make it kind of pricey. It entirely depends on the state. The search results will usually give you the full legal name of the business and the name and address of its registered agent (in case you need to have it served). More detailed searches can also reveal the business's status with the state, the names of the officers, and more. For the purpose of drafting a contract, though, you'll usually just need the legal name.

Standard Clauses

Contracts vary, of course, depending on their nature, purpose, and content. But you'll find that in most business contracts (including sales contracts, leases, loan agreements, and others), there are a few standard clauses, usually toward the end of the contract, after the "meat and potatoes." These clauses are designed to tie up loose ends, prevent miscommunication in the future, and set a standard for further discussions.

I'll briefly list the most common ones:

▸ **Integration Clause**—This clause clarifies that *only* what is written in the agreement actually counts. This way, if something was discussed and settled, but not included in the written contract for some reason, it's clear that it's *not* part of the final agreement. This is useful if the parties discussed an issue and agreed to it, but also agreed to postpone it until a future date or a separate deal.

▸ **Successors and Assignees Clause**—This clause defines the rights of all parties involved, in the event that one of the original parties assigns or sells his rights while the contract is still enforceable. In other words, does the contract carry over to the new owners? And does one party have to get permission from the other party to assign or sell his rights to the contract? These are questions that can be answered in the successors and assignees clause.

▶ **Communications and Notices Clause**—This clause will help the parties determine how they'll communicate about the contract going forward. This includes providing mailing addresses, email addresses, and rules for important notifications.

▶ **Modifications Clause**—The parties should decide from the beginning how future modifications and changes will be made to the agreement.

▶ **Governing Law Clause**—Particularly important if you and the other party are registered and/or do business in different states, this clause specifies which state's laws will govern the contract. If both parties are registered in the same state, then that state's laws will govern.

▶ **Waiver Clause**—If a party fails to enforce a contractual right, it can be interpreted to mean that he waived it, or gave it up. A waiver clause means that both parties agree that rights are not permanently waived in this manner; that way everybody has a fair chance to enforce his rights under the contract.

Signing Contracts

This topic is especially important. Contracts are enforceable *only* if they're signed by the correct parties and in the proper format. The signature, much like the name listed on the contract, determines the validity of the contract and who is actually liable.

Legal Persons

Not just anybody can sign a contract, especially in the business world.

First, understand that only "legal persons" can be a party to a contract. This can mean two different things: It can literally mean a person, as in a human being, legally known as an "individual." Or it can mean a formally filed business entity.

Recall from earlier chapters that formally created business entities have their own rights. So, corporations and LLCs have the ability to enter into contracts. Also recall that this is part of your corporate-veil protection. The creation of a formal legal entity means that your small business is a separate entity from you, and the business itself can enter into its own agreements separately and apart from you, the individual.

Keep in mind, of course, that if you operate as a sole proprietor, then you are the business and the business is you. You, the individual, will sign any contractual agreements and you'll be personally responsible for the debts and liabilities. This is true even if you use a DBA or fictitious name. For example, if you operate as a sole proprietor cleaning commercial buildings at night, your signature line might look like this:

Sally P. May, d/b/a May's Maids
Sole Proprietor

Formal entities, on the other hand, can enter into their own contracts, but a human being still has to sign on their behalf, of course. This person is known as an *agent* and the correct agent's signature is of utmost importance. The proper signature will make it clear that the agent is signing "on behalf of" the business and not as an individual or sole proprietor. If May's Maids were actually registered as a Wyoming LLC, then the signature line might look like this:

May's Maids, LLC

By: _____
    Sally P. May, Manager

Who Signs?

This brings me to my next point. *Who* actually signs on behalf of a formal business entity is important. Again, it can't be just anybody. In order to act and sign on a business's behalf, the signing agent must actually have authority to do so. For example, salesmen often have the authority to contractually sign on new clients, within certain parameters. But those same salesmen probably won't have the authority to sign a new lease agreement for the company. That type of authority will likely fall to a manager, partner, or officer.

Your small business's signing authority should be spelled out in your partnership agreement, operating agreement, or bylaws, depending on which entity structure you choose. For example, your corporation's bylaws may define the signing authority of each officer position, such as who can sign minor contracts versus who can sign major contracts. Similarly, if you operate an LLC, your operating agreement should clarify whether all managers have equal signing power or if one holds more authority over the others. Point being, your organizational documents should define who has the authority to sign contracts on behalf of your small business and what they have the authority to sign for. It's often easier to list exclusions to signing authority rather than list everything that an agent *can* sign for.

On the other hand, if you're drafting a contract for review by a third party, you'll want to confirm who has signing authority within that organization. This serves one very important purpose: you want to make sure that the person you're negotiating and doing business with actually has the authority to do so. If you sign an agreement with the corporate VP and later find out that he had no authority to make a deal with you, you may find that your contract is completely null and void.

Signature Examples

Here, I've listed examples of contract signatures for various different types of entities.

General partnership:
Rogers & Rogers

By: _____
            Phillip L. Rogers, General Partner

Corporation:
The ABC, Inc.

By: _____
            Allen B. Cool, President

Corporation with a fictitious name:
The ABC, Inc. d/b/a Alphabet Soup

By: _____
            Allen B. Cool, President

Limited Liability Company with a fictitious name:
ABC Marketing, LLC d/b/a Creative Marketing Solutions

By: _____
            Michael B. Bowman, Manager

Limited partnership:
Black & Blue, LP

By: _____
     Janet B. Blue, General Partner

Limited partnership with a corporate general partner:
Black & Blue, LP

By: Sands, Inc., its general partner

By: _____
     Ginger S. Sands, President

Templates vs. Attorneys

Last but not least, let's quickly discuss the topic of using a contract template versus having an attorney draft one for you. This almost entirely depends on what the contract is for.

Major contracts, for example, such as purchasing a new warehouse, buying out another company, or contracting with a new supplier, should be drafted, or at least reviewed, by an attorney. These types of contracts aren't something you're going to deal with on a daily, weekly, or even monthly basis. In other words, you won't be familiar with them. They're likely to contain complex nuances, unique clauses, and unfamiliar legal terms, all of which can leave you very vulnerable if you don't completely understand what you're agreeing to.

On the other hand, there are certain contractual issues that won't necessarily require an attorney's touch every single time. For example, your small business may use a standard contract to engage new clients, or a certain set of agreements when you hire new employees. As long as an attorney has drafted the original contract templates, then it should be acceptable for you to use the templates when signing on new clients or employees, if you periodically have them reviewed for changes with the law. Always be sure to fill in the blanks, update the date, add the correct party names, and adjust the signature lines as needed.

A few words of caution with templates, though. First, you should have them reviewed by an attorney on at least a biannual basis, to ensure that they're still in accordance with all current laws. Second, anytime that a client, employee, or third party requests that something be adjusted on one of your standard contracts, I would suggest running it by your attorney first. Contracts are tricky things, and even the slightest adjustments can have a tremendous impact on your liabilities, obligations, and rights.

10

Meetings and Record Keeping

As a recovering litigation attorney, I can't emphasize enough the importance of running proper meetings and keeping accurate records of them. If your business is ever audited or sued, your records and meeting minutes will be some of the first things that you'll have to relinquish to the opposing side or auditor. The quality of these records can either make you or break you, save you or forsake you when it comes to protecting your corporate veil. Here, we'll discuss formal meetings and important decisions, and how to record them effectively. Keep in mind that most of these meetings and decisions will be unique to corporations or LLCs. Sole proprietorships and partnerships won't have these formalities and rules. I have included an appendix of sample meetings for your convenience at the end of this book.

Shareholder Meetings

We learned in Chapter 6 that launching a successful corporation begins with an organizational meeting to make several key decisions about the future of your business. We also discussed in detail the importance of properly documenting the minutes for that meeting. If you operate as a corporation, though, that first official meeting, and the important decisions made there, will be far from being your last.

All corporations are required by law to hold at least one shareholder meeting per year. Known as the *Annual Shareholder Meeting*, this meeting is a strict statutory requirement so it should never be disregarded, even if you just hold the meeting as a legal formality. The main goal of the annual shareholder meeting is to nominate and vote on the next board of directors, although you may include other issues on the agenda as needed. Your shareholders will have to decide if they want to reaffirm the current directors or elect and sanction new ones. Remember that you'll have to honor state laws, your corporate bylaws, and your articles of incorporation when making this decision.

Your corporate bylaws will specify which date the annual meeting should be held, as well as the time and place. While it's important to try and honor this date as much as possible, it's not absolutely necessary. Life happens and sometimes the annual meeting just can't be held exactly as planned. But if the annual shareholder meeting does need to be moved to a different date, time, or place, it should be called the *Substitute Annual Meeting* instead and notice should be given.

Some issues can't wait for the annual meeting. If an important shareholder matter arises before the annual meeting is scheduled, a *Special Shareholder Meeting* should be called. For example, a special meeting may be called to make an amendment to the bylaws, vote on a time-sensitive merger, or make changes to the way stocks are issued. These special meetings are more common in larger corporations than small businesses, but they do happen and you should be prepared for them to come up from time to time.

Meeting Formalities

Of utmost importance to your corporate-veil protection is following certain formalities before, during, and after your shareholder meetings. These formalities prove that your shareholder meetings are legitimate meetings where decisions are being made by the shareholders as a group and not just you, as an individual. First, the law requires that shareholders be given an official notice that a share-holder meeting has been called. Remember, one of the few shareholder rights is the right to vote, so it's critical that you give your shareholders the chance to exercise this right. At your organizational meeting, you and the original directors will determine how much of a notice will be required. The notice should be no less than ten days prior to a meeting and no more than sixty days prior. The standard notice is thirty days for an annual meeting and ten days for a special meeting. Be sure to check the laws in your state of formation, though.

In preparation for a shareholder meeting, a *meeting folder* and *meeting summary sheet* will help to document and organize the purpose, date, and time of the meeting. While there is generally no legal requirement for these documents, the habit of preparing them can serve as a record that you are following everything that is a legal formality. If they're well organized, they can also be helpful to your corporate secretary or treasurer, who can pull and review the records as needed.

Another important legal formality is that of a quorum. A quorum is a requirement that a certain number of shareholders be present at a meeting in order for any votes and decisions to be valid. In other words, if a shareholder meeting doesn't have enough shareholders in attendance to meet the quorum, then the meeting has to be adjourned and rescheduled and no votes can be taken. Each state has its own quorum requirements. Some states require that 25 percent of shareholders be present at a meeting, while others require that one-third of the shareholders be present. Quorum requirements will also come from your bylaws, though. At your organizational meeting, you and your initial shareholders will need to decide if you want your quorum to be stricter than the state's minimum requirements or if you're simply going to follow the requirements set by law. For example, your state law may require that 25 percent of all shareholders be present for a shareholder meeting, but your bylaws may state that at least half of all shareholders be present. In that case, your bylaws' standards would need to be honored.

Finally, in chapter 6, we discussed the organizational meeting minutes. The formalities and format used for those minutes should be followed at each and every shareholder meeting for the life of your corporation. Your corporate secretary should keep a thorough record of what was discussed and said during every shareholder meeting, then record the minutes in your corporate binder. Hard copies, as well as digital copies, should be kept, just in case.

Changing or Amending Bylaws

One of the few decisions specifically left to shareholders is the task of amending your corporate bylaws. Remember that your bylaws are a contract, of sorts, between the shareholders and the corporation. Any deviation from that contract is a violation of the law and a threat to your corporate veil. In order to amend or change the contract, the shareholders have to hold an official vote and follow certain procedures to make any amendments valid.

Usually, amendment proposals are introduced by the board of directors. The board works directly with your officers, so they know, better than anybody, when the bylaws need to be adjusted to meet your corporation's growing and changing needs. But they can't amend the bylaws on their own. So the board of directors will draft a resolution for the proposed change and then contact the shareholders to call a special shareholder meeting.

All of the formalities to call and notify shareholders of a special meeting will need to be fulfilled. At the meeting itself, the shareholders will discuss the proposed amendment and then take a vote. A unanimous vote is generally not required to amend the bylaws, unless your bylaws specifically state that. Usually, a majority vote is all that's needed. If the proposed amendment is approved, the bylaws will officially be amended by your corporate secretary.

Board of Director Meetings

Just like the shareholders, the board of directors must act as one to make important decisions. When the board makes decisions as a group, it protects your corporate veil and serves as proof that the corporation is operating as a business entity, and not just an individual. (I sound like a broken record, right? But this is what it's all about.)

While shareholder meetings are generally marked by brief conversation and a vote, board of director meetings should include quite a bit more discussion and debate. Remember, your board of directors will have a lot more authority than your shareholders. The board is responsible for the overall direction and management of the business, so their decisions and votes should be thoroughly discussed, honestly debated, and taken very seriously. This is true whether the board is just you, your wife, and two nephews meeting at the office, or whether you have fifteen board members from across the country meeting in a hotel conference room.

Unlike your shareholders, your board of directors should meet regularly throughout the year. The law requires an annual meeting, but most boards meet quarterly or monthly as well. These meetings are known as *Special Meetings*. The frequency will depend entirely on the size and standing of your business. If your corporation is small and finances are steady, then a quarterly meeting may suffice to review the quarterly budget and make minor adjustments. However, if your corporation is growing, expanding, changing, or struggling, then a monthly or even weekly meeting may be helpful, at least while you navigate the changes and rough waters. And, of course, a special meeting may be called if an important matter arises that needs to be discussed right away.

Board of Director Meeting Formalities

Because your board will be responsible for more decisions, the formalities and meeting requirements are a bit different.

Notice Requirements

Notice requirements for board of directors meetings are not nearly as strict as the shareholders. Technically, your board of directors can't make decisions at a meeting unless an official notice of the meeting was given. "Notice," however, usually just means that the board of directors was notified, in writing, at least ten days before the meeting, even if it was just a simple email. The reason for the relaxed notification requirements is that directors, theoretically, are more involved in the business operations. In other words, serving on the board is more of a job and responsibility than simply owning shares, so board members are expected to devote their time to regular meetings and should be anticipating them, without the need for an extended notification. Nonetheless, don't get complacent and skip the written notification requirement. Usually, a secretary, assistant, or chairman of the board, can send out an email or memo, or add the meeting to a mutual calendar.

Quorum

Your board will have a quorum requirement, just like your shareholders. However, your articles of incorporation can call for a different number. When needed, there is also a simple way around a quorum. Let's say that your board of directors consists of seven members but only three showed up to a meeting. The meeting could still take place, to include votes, if the four absent board members were willing to sign a document approving the meeting and any votes that took place. In other words, with the absent board members' written consent, the quorum can be omitted and the meeting decisions can be validated. This can be very helpful if a decision needs to be made in a timely manner but you can't get all of your board members together in time.

Meeting Conduct and Agenda

The way you conduct your board meetings is also an important consideration. While there are no specific legal requirements, a structured board meeting with a standard agenda and order can provide an organized record of your meetings, which may prove invaluable if your business is ever audited or sued. We typically recommend the following basic format:

1. Call to Order—Usually by the board chairman, president, or CEO

2. Announcement that quorum has been met

3. Reading and approval of previous meeting minutes—Usually performed by your secretary or equivalent

4. Reports from officers and/or committees

5. Discussion of unfinished business

6. Election of officers (if needed)

7. Declaration of dividends (if applicable)

8. New business items to be discussed

9. Business adjourned

Motions and Resolutions

Yet another important procedure at your board meetings will be the handling of motions and resolutions. Very simply, a motion is a proposed idea or official suggestion, and a resolution is a conclusive decision to accept and implement the proposed idea.

Let's say that your treasurer proposes that your business move all its accounts to a different bank, in order to take advantage of better rates and benefits. This proposal would be added to the agenda. Your treasurer would present his proposed idea and then your board may proceed to discuss the pros and cons. After the discussion, your treasurer would make an official "motion" to take action on the proposed idea and move the business's accounts. If another member of the board speaks up to "second" the motion, then the proposal will be voted on. If none of your other board members second the motion, then it will be dismissed without a vote.

If the motion is seconded, voted on, and passed, then it's known as a resolution. So if the treasurer's motion is seconded and the majority of your directors vote yes, then the board, as a whole, has made a resolution to move your company's accounts to a new bank. Your secretary will need to diligently record every step of this process for the meeting minutes, which will be discussed in more detail in just a moment.

From a legal perspective, official resolutions aren't always necessary in order for your board to make a binding decision. However, resolutions are effective, because they create a contract-like agreement that will help to eliminate misunderstandings and disagreements down the road. In other words, when your secretary records the results of a vote as a "resolution," it provides an indisputable record that the board came to an agreement and made a binding decision.

That said, there are a handful of times when an official resolution *will* actually be required. First, the law or your bylaws may demand it. For example, if your board votes to make a distribution to the shareholders, it has to be an official resolution, because the law requires distributions to be made based on an official resolution by a board. Second, if a proposed idea or change will necessarily result in the filing of a certificate or other recorded document of some kind, then an official resolution will be required. If your board votes to make an amendment to the articles of incorporation, for example, a resolution will be required because the articles will have to be amended and re-recorded with the state.

As a general rule, a resolution may not be required but is still advisable if:

- ▶ The issue is meant to be a permanent rule change,

- ▶ The decision will have a significant impact on the business, or

- ▶ It's an issue that will be referred to again in the future.

In other words, unless it's a small matter, a resolution is beneficial and therefore recommended.

Meeting Minutes

We've talked a lot about meeting minutes sporadically throughout the book, but here I'll provide some specifics.

First, meeting minutes are not actually a legal requirement in all states. However, that doesn't negate their importance to your corporate veil or record keeping. Every board meeting (and shareholder meeting, for that matter) should be diligently recorded by the secretary. The minutes should include a copy of the agenda, explanations of what was presented by the officers and committees, notes about discussions, who said what, how each board member voted on each motion, and notes about any other conversations that took place during the scope of the meeting. Following the meeting, your secretary should type up a clean and official version of the minutes to be placed in the corporate binder.

Furthermore, once the meeting minutes are actually recorded in the binder, directors do have the right to make corrections to them in the future. This is why, at every meeting, the minutes from the last meeting should be read aloud. Your secretary will be only human, after all, and it's possible that he or she may incorrectly record a comment or a vote. After reading the minutes, board members can speak up to make any necessary corrections. Once the corrections have been made, the minutes can be "approved" by the board. This signifies that the board agrees with what was written and the minutes become an official record.

Removal, Resignation, and Replacement of Directors

Your elected directors won't necessarily be permanent members of your board. Typically, they serve one-year terms and will either be re-elected or replaced by your shareholders at the annual meeting. Other times, a board member may be removed mid-year because of issues such as fraud or gross misconduct. And, of course, board members may sometimes decide to resign, for one reason or another. The processes of removing, resigning, and replacing directors will be discussed in more detail next.

Before we move on, understand that when you have a vacancy on your board, it doesn't mean that business comes to a halt. Your board will continue to meet and vote on the important matters of your business. At the same time, though, the vacancy will need to be filled as soon as possible.

Each year, when your shareholders meet, their main goal will be to elect and vote for the next year's directors. If they're happy with the performance of the current directors, they may re-elect and appoint them with a two-thirds vote. If the directors' performance has been unsatisfactory, the shareholders may elect and appoint new directors. Also keep in mind that the board does not get elected and appointed as a whole body. Each board member is considered individually. After your first year of business, your shareholders may re-appoint three of your five board members, for example, and replace the other two.

State laws also allow the removal of a board member, which can happen anytime between the annual meetings. If your shareholders wish to remove a board member, they can do so without cause. This means that they don't necessarily have to have a specific reason. If they decide, through a majority vote, to remove a board member, then the removal will be valid. However, if a board member needs to be removed "for cause," then the shareholders have to vote to remove the member. "For cause" means that there is a specific reason to remove the board member. This usually means that a board member has acted fraudulently or violated his duties of loyalty and care to the company. When, and if that happens, your shareholders can vote, by a majority, to remove that member.

Finally, directors may leave your board by resigning. This is allowed, of course, because you can't force somebody to serve on your board. However, they do have to follow a process to officially and legally resign. First, the resigning member should submit a written notice to your board of directors or the president. The written notification isn't a rigid requirement but, like everything else, it creates a written record that eliminates arguments or misunderstandings. The board member's written resignation should include the date that his resignation is effective, but he doesn't have to provide his reason for resigning. On the effective date of the resignation, you will have a vacant seat on your board. Just as we discussed earlier, only the shareholders can fill that vacancy. They may need to call a special meeting to elect a new board member and vote on the appointment.

Meetings for your LLC

From a legal perspective, regular meetings held by the managers and/or members of your LLC are not usually a strict obligation. If you recall from Chapter 7, however, the law hasn't exactly caught up to the growth of LLCs. In other words, just because the law doesn't require formal meetings (yet) doesn't mean that you shouldn't hold them. Just like a corporation, an LLC's corporate veil is protected by evidence that the business is operating as a separate legal entity with rules, restrictions, and regulations. So, just like a corporation, organized business meetings and carefully written records can prove that your LLC is a legit operation and not just an alter ego.

Your LLC's operating agreement will likely provide more guidance for your meetings than the law will. Your operating agreement should require an annual meeting of the managers and/or members, as well as provide guidance on how to call special meetings as needed throughout the year.

How you structure your LLC will determine, in many ways, how your meetings should be run and what issues will be discussed.

Member-Managed Meetings and Decisions

Recall that a member-managed LLC means that all of your members will work collectively to manage the business together. In other words, all of your members will be directly involved in the management of the business. If your LLC is structured this way, then your meetings and important decisions will be pretty straightforward. Essentially, your members will need to meet, discuss, and vote on all important issues as a group. No one person will have the authority to make a decision that will have a lasting or profound effect on the future or overall financial standing of the business. For example, if you operate a small accounting firm as an LLC with your two brothers, then you will likely be a member-managed LLC. As a group, you will collectively meet to discuss financial and organizational matters, such as paying off debts, leasing new office space, hiring employees, or bringing in new members.

Recall, though, that members may serve in certain positions or roles and be given authority to make related decisions without the approval of the other members. These positions, such as CEO, managing member, or director, should have clear job descriptions within your operating agreement. For example, one of your brothers (a member) may serve as the marketing director, so he may have the authority to make simple adjustments to the business's website or hire a freelance copywriter to create a short ebook without consulting the other members first. But, as I said, job descriptions for various member positions should be very clear. Anything not assigned to a specific member should be left to the group to decide together at a formal meeting.

Manager-Managed Meetings and Decisions

If your business is structured as a manager-managed LLC, then decision-making authority will be a bit more complex. Your members will essentially serve in the role of investors; meaning that they'll have some ownership of the business but they won't necessarily be directly involved in the day-to-day activities. Your members' decision-making authority, then, would be limited to the following types of issues:

▶ Electing and appointing managers,

▶ Amending the operating agreement or articles of incorporation,

▶ Approving loans or real estate leases and purchases,

▶ Affirming a new member, and

▶ Continuing or dissolving the LLC.

A simple rule of thumb is to also include your members in decisions that will affect the overall profitability and financial status of the business. Let's say that your small interior design business has a growing list of clients. You have two managers, yourself and one other, and you both feel the need to lease the small, empty office space next door in order to create a new reception area and hire a full-time receptionist. While the law may not require you to seek permission from your two non-manager members, it would definitely be advisable to do so anyway. Leasing that space and hiring a new employee would be a significant cost to the business. All of this would affect your business's bottom line, which is what your members are most concerned with. By holding a meeting to allow your members to discuss and vote on this issue, you'll be creating a valuable record of their approval, which will reduce the risk of a lawsuit or dispute later on. It will also serve as proof that you're not making major decisions on your own.

Electing Managers

As was noted, if you operate a manager-managed LLC, one of your members' key roles will be to elect and appoint managers. At the annual members meeting, they'll need to elect, vote for, and officially appoint the managers for the upcoming year. Typically, the annual managers meeting will be held directly following the members meeting. Your newly elected managers will formally accept their positions and then discuss issues for the upcoming year. Remember, as a small business, most of your members will likely serve as managers, so these annual meetings can typically be run back-to-back and at the same location.

But it's important to maintain the formalities of separating the meetings and holding votes.

Real Meetings vs. Paper-Only Meetings

Because LLC laws have fewer meeting requirements, it is acceptable to hold a "paper-only meeting" for members and/or managers, depending on the circumstances. Paper-only meetings are beneficial if a simple decision needs to be made or if it's clear that most of the members/managers have unofficially agreed on a particular issue.

The decision to take out a small loan, for example, may have been considered via email, and all of the members have expressed that they're on board. Or, at the last manager meeting, they may have discussed the possibility of hiring a full-time shipping and receiving manager for the night crew. No official decision was made but now, three months later, it's become clear to the director that the position needs to be filled. She may call each of the other managers for verbal approval and then go ahead with the hiring process. In either case, an official paper record would still need to be established. A set of minutes would need to be prepared as if a "real" meeting had occurred.

"Real" meetings, on the other hand, are sometimes a necessity. If the matter to be discussed is controversial, complex, requires a full debate, or will have a profound effect on the future of the company, then your members and/or managers should hold a real meeting, together as a group. These meetings should have all the formalities of a corporate meeting, to include a timely notice, an agenda and order of conduct, and motions and resolutions.

Closing a Business

Last, but not least, when the time comes to end your business operations, it will be a little more complex than simply closing the doors and selling off the equipment. Ending a corporation, LLC, or other formally filed business entity will mean more procedures, forms, and records. This, as you may imagine, will help to establish a legal paper trail proving that the business's legal obligations were met and that all loose ends were tied before you officially ended your business operations. It's a critical final step in the protection of your corporate veil.

Corporations

A corporation can be closed through a process called dissolution, which is initiated by the board of directors. First, the board of directors votes and passes a resolution for dissolution. The shareholders then vote to approve the dissolution, and the corporation enters into a stage known as "winding up the business." The winding-up stage is the process of selling any remaining assets, paying off existing creditors, and distributing any remaining funds to the shareholders.

After the winding up is complete, dissolution becomes the legal process of terminating the corporation's existence at the local, state, and federal levels. In other words, you need to notify the government that your corporation is no longer an operating, functioning entity. The corporation will need to surrender any business licenses with the city and county at the local level. At the state level, the corporation will need to file a dissolution form with the secretary of state, usually called the "Articles of Dissolution." This is to ensure that the state will cease billing the yearly filing fees and to notify the public that the corporation is no longer in business.

The corporation will also need to notify the IRS of the dissolution. A final tax return must be filed for the closing year of the corporation. The corporate tax return form has a box near the top of the front page to indicate that it's the final return. The corporation must file the final employment tax return and make the final employment tax deposits for the employees. Upon completing the steps of dissolution, the corporation will cease to exist.

LLCs

The process of closing an LLC is very similar to the process of closing a corporation. The members will need to vote and approve the dissolution of the LLC. Most operating agreements will outline the preferred procedure for the LLC's dissolution.

Before filing the dissolution of the LLC with the state and federal government, the LLC will need to pay the remaining creditors, distribute any remaining funds to the members, and close the bank accounts. The LLC will need to surrender any business licenses at the city and county levels, and then file Articles of Dissolution with the state for the LLC. Just like the dissolution of a corporation, the

LLC will also need to notify the IRS of its closure by filing the final tax return for the LLC. The LLC no longer exists after the regulatory filings are accepted.

CHAPTER

11

▬▬▬

Accounting, Bookkeeping, and Getting Paid

Once your small business is up and running, money will be the name of the game: earning it, balancing it, and spending it wisely. After all, nobody starts a business so that they can go broke, right? But how you track and spend your money will affect more than just your pocketbook. It will also have a profound impact on your corporate-veil protection.

I certainly don't expect you to be a financial expert by the end of this chapter. In fact, this is one of those areas of small business ownership where you may need to solicit some professional help. (We'll talk about that, too!) But every small business owner should at least have an understanding of basic bookkeeping and accounting terms, methods, and principles. Even if you don't actually manage these tasks yourself, you still need to recognize what you're looking at when you review your balance sheets, ledgers, and profit & loss statements. Here, I will give you that foundational understanding. This will help you keep a better finger on the financial pulse of your entity.

Bookkeeping vs. Accounting

The first order of business is to clear up a common misunderstanding. Bookkeeping and accounting are not synonymous; they're two separate processes, but they do work hand in hand.

Bookkeeping is a form of record keeping. It's the method of recording your business's daily money matters; how much money comes in and how much goes out.

Accounting, on the other hand, is the broader and more complex practice of interpreting your bookkeeping records and measuring the overall financial health of your business. Accounting can tell you if you're making enough money to pay your creditors and employees, if you have too much debt, and what your net profit is for any given time period. It will also tell you how much you can pay yourself. And that, of course, is the part we all look forward to.

Because they require two different skill levels, it's important to note that bookkeepers aren't necessarily accountants, and accountants aren't necessarily bookkeepers. True accountants require special education and training, as well as official certification, so they're often unwilling to do the simpler tasks of bookkeeping. Bookkeepers, on the other hand, don't usually have the necessary education to perform accounting procedures. In large accounting firms, bookkeepers work under accountants, and generally make less money.

Who handles *your* bookkeeping and accounting will depend on a number of different factors. If you're a sole proprietor, you can probably manage your accounting and bookkeeping with a simple software program. There are dozens of reputable ones available. Partnerships, too, can often manage their own bookkeeping and accounting this way.

If you're operating a formal business entity, however, then your finances will be more complex. Corporations and LLCs are subject to more rules, regulations, and statutes than sole proprietors or simple partnerships, as we've been discussing throughout the entirety of this book. These regulations will extend to your bookkeeping and accounting practices. Being able to stay in compliance financially is an incredibly important aspect of protecting your corporate veil, especially when it comes to the IRS. So soliciting some professional financial help can be a wise investment for your business.

Often, small business owners hire a bookkeeper to work in-house (or use software themselves), but hire an outside accountant to help prepare tax returns and provide guidance for financial reviews and tricky transactions. You may find that your small business requires a full-time accountant, while you handle the bookkeeping part yourself. Or, you might hire a flexible accountant to do the job of both bookkeeper and accountant. Whatever you decide, it will entirely depend on your business needs, your own personal skill set, and the complexity of your business's finances. You certainly shouldn't be afraid to solicit some help in this area, though.

Bookkeeping 101

Bookkeeping may be the simpler sister to accounting, but it provides a foundation for all of your other financial records. If your bookkeeping isn't right, then your accounting and taxes won't be right, either. And because taxes and accounting have to comply with strict state and federal laws, bookkeeping should be done, well, by the book. If your business is ever audited, your bookkeeping records and methods will be thoroughly scrutinized. If the IRS can't tell where your business's money is coming from or how it's being spent, it's going to look highly suspect and become a serious threat to your corporate-veil protection.

Key Terms

Before I go into detail about bookkeeping methods, let's go over some standard bookkeeping terms.

- ▶ **Revenue**—The money your business brings in
  - This includes sales, payments made by clients, rental payments if your business owns property, etc.

- ▶ **Expenses**—The money your business pays out
  - This includes payroll, utility bills, supplies, transportation, lease payments, marketing expenses, etc.

- ▶ **Profit**—This is what's left over after you subtract your expenses from your revenue
  - This is *not* the same as your personal income from the business.

- ▶ **General Ledger**—A record book for recording all business revenues and expenses in chronological order

- ▶ **Journal**—A way of recording transactions for different areas of your business

  - ◆ For example, you may keep one journal to track transactions for the service side of your business and a separate journal for the sale of goods.

General Ledgers vs. Journals

The use of one general ledger is usually better suited for small businesses that only offer one type of service and/ or good. For example, if you're a fitness instructor offering classes at the local recreation center, and operating as a simple partnership with your sister, you can probably keep just one general ledger to track all of your revenue and expenses.

But if you open a gym and offer fitness classes, personal training, workout equipment, and apparel, then you may be better suited to keep two different journals to separate your goods from your services. This can help you to see exactly where your money is coming from and where it's being spent. For example, this may help you determine that the sale of workout apparel isn't profitable because it is costing you more money than it is earning. Or, you may be able to recognize that your group fitness classes account for 75 percent of your revenue so you can capitalize on that fact and offer more group classes.

If you keep more than one journal, the records from the journals should still be copied into one general ledger. Instead of updating the ledger daily, though, you can update it weekly, monthly, or quarterly. You would simply take the totals from all of your journals and enter them into the ledger. This will allow you to see the total of your revenues and expenses, from all of the different areas of your business.

In sum, a general ledger gives you a big picture of all the incoming and outgoing money from your business. Journals, on the other hand, allow you to break your business down into different areas and revenue streams so that you can fully analyze what's profitable and what's not.

Single-Entry vs. Double-Entry

The way you make entries to your ledger and journals can also differ. The two most common methods are single-entry and double-entry. Without going into unnecessary details, I'll explain the basics of both. Remember, the goal here isn't to make you an expert; you just need a foundational understanding of how this all works and how it relates to your corporate veil.

The single-entry method is most popular among sole proprietors and small partnerships because it's simple and doesn't require any kind of special training or education. Anybody can use this method but it can still be very effective and accurate, especially for simple small businesses.

Essentially, the single-entry method means that you'll make one entry in your ledger for each transaction, such as the example below of a sole proprietor:

DATE	TRANSACTION	REVENUE	EXPENSE	BALANCE
March 3, 2020	Beginning weekly balance			$5,345
March 3, 2020	Monthly lease		$955	
March 3, 2020	Supply purchase		$175	
March 3, 2020	Networking group monthly dues		$45	
March 3, 2020	New client deposit: Jim Beaux	$500		
March 4, 2020	Payment from client: Mary Jones	$750		
March 5, 2020	Payment from client: Dave Smith	$1,100		
March 6, 2020	Software update		$350	
March 7, 2020	Ending weekly balance			$6,170

The double-entry method, on the other hand, requires more training and skill but it also provides a more accurate record. Accountants typically use the double-entry method. If you operate as an LLC or corporation, or offer a wide variety of goods and services, you'll likely need to use this method. We'll discuss it in more detail in just a moment.

Accounting 101

If your business operates as a formal business entity, has employees, offers multiple goods or services, or has a lot of cash and credit moving around, then accounting will become all that much more important. First, when it comes to your business taxes, every penny counts. If your accounting is accurate, you should be able to take advantage of small business write-offs and possibly even save money on your returns. And second, accounting procedures that strictly follow accounting rules and regulations will do wonders for your corporate veil if you're ever audited or sued. If the IRS or courts can easily see how your business was earning and spending money, and that your personal finances were clearly uninvolved, then your corporate veil should remain heartily intact.

Key Terms

Now it's time to add a few more key terms to your financial index.

► **Cash**—The amount of unrestricted cash that you have on hand

► **Credit**—Money earned that hasn't been received yet

  • For example, if you billed a client but he hasn't yet paid.

► **Asset**—The items that your business owns outright and that have value

- This includes cash in bank accounts, as well as items like inventory, furniture, and computers.

► **Liability**—Money that your business owes to creditors or debtors

- This may include rent, credit cards, business loans, and utility bills.

► **Equity**—The difference between assets and liabilities

- This amount represents the total value of your business.

Profit & Loss Statements and Balance Sheets

Two of the most important accounting logs your business will ever keep will be your profit & loss statements (P&L) and your balance sheets. A P&L is simply a summary of your business profits and losses for a given period of time. For example, your accountant may prepare a P&L at the end of every quarter by subtracting your expenses from your revenues, as they were recorded on your general ledger. This will tell you what your business's net profit was for that particular quarter.

The example below shows the fitness instructors' P&L statement for the month of January:

Income	
Sales	$680
Services	$3,475
Total Income	**$3,155**
Expenses	
Lease	$800
Supplies	$525
Marketing	$100
Total Expenses	**$1,425**
Net Profit (Income — Expenses)	**$2,730**

Again, this is an overly simplified example but it should give you an idea of how a P&L works.

A balance sheet, on the other hand, shows you the overall financial health of your business at an exact point in time. It gives you a snapshot, so to speak, of how much you owe, how much you're owed, and how much you have, at any given moment. It's a step beyond just what your profits and losses were. The most important part of the balance sheet is that it actually balances. Accountants use a formula for balance sheets: Assets = Liabilities + Equity.

Below is an example of the fitness instructors' balance sheet as of December 31, 2016:

Assets	
Bank Accounts	
USAA Checking	$6,455
Wells Fargo Business Savings	$1,650
Other Assets	
Inventory	$650
Equipment	$8,321
Total Assets	**$17,076**

Liabilities	
USAA Business Loan	$10,499
Total Liabilities	**$10,499**
Equity	
Opening Equity Balance	$5,917
Net Income	$660
Total Equity	**$6,567**

Total Liabilities and Equity	**$17,076**

Double-Entry Method

This, by the way, is where the double-entry method comes into play. This method means that for each transaction, two separate entries are made in your ledger or journal, instead of one. One entry is made as a debit and one as a credit. It's a cause-and-effect situation. The money will come out of one account and go into another. This is how your balance sheet will actually balance. As usual, the best way to explain this is through an example.

Let's say that you're a web developer who just purchased ad space in the local chamber of commerce monthly newsletter. The advertising fee would look something like this as a double-entry in your ledger:

ACCOUNT	DEBIT	CREDIT
Assets/Checking Account	$450	
Expenses/ Advertising		$450

In this case, you spent $450 from your checking account, which would decrease your assets. At the same time, you increased your expenses by $450, so that gets recorded as a credit to your expenses account. Keep in mind that this is another very simplified example, but it should give you a general idea of how it works. The point of double-entry is to balance the accounts on your balance sheets.

Types of Accounts

Finally, in order to get the full accounting picture, we need to discuss the concept of having more than one account. This should clear up any lingering questions you have about how the balance sheet works.

In order to balance your books, you need to have separate "accounts" for the various activities of your business. Most small businesses can operate with five accounts: assets, liabilities, equity, income, and expenses. (You should recognize these terms by now!) The point is that you're separating each of these activities, or areas of your business. It's important to note here that these "accounts" won't be actual bank accounts. It's just a way of visually separating and categorizing your different business transactions. Sometimes it helps to think of these accounts as separate files in a filing cabinet. When money is taken from one file it has to be moved to another. The income and expense files, or accounts, will be used to complete your profit & loss statements. Your asset, liability, and equity accounts will be used to complete your balance sheets.

Your head may be spinning a little bit at this point, but don't be dismayed. Your finances will become clearer in time and with practice. Don't forget, there are plenty of software programs to help you with this aspect of your business. And, I repeat, you should never underestimate the power of having a team of well-trained bookkeepers and tax professionals on your side. Trained professionals will play a valuable role in protecting your corporate veil, especially when it comes to your bookkeeping and accounting.

Pay Day!

Last but not least, let's talk about payday. Every small business owner dreams of setting her own salary, and it may very well be one of the many benefits that drew you to small business ownership in the first place.

Hold that thought, though, while we go over some commonsense and legal matters when it comes to paying your own salary.

First, how you pay yourself will depend on whether or not you play an active role in the business, and what type of entity you operate as. In most cases, you'll receive income from the business as a *distribution or draw*. The difference is mostly tax related. A draw is not considered a business expense. It's simply what business owners pull from their businesses. You'll notice, in the chart below, that this only applies to sole proprietors and single-member LLCs, which means that there are very few restrictions. If you operate as a sole proprietor or SMLLC, you can draw a salary from the business any time you see fit. Just be sure to use your common sense and math skills. In other words, don't take a draw if it means that the business is going to bounce a check or miss a payment.

A distributive share, on the other hand, is a bit more restrictive. You'll notice that distributive shares mostly apply to the more formal business entities that offer corporate-veil protection. This should be your clue that the way you pay yourself a distribution matters. Your operating agreement or partnership agreement should actually specify how distributions should be made. This means that you can't just distribute money to yourself whenever you feel like it. You, your partners, members, and/

or shareholders will have to follow the legalities, as well as the distribution rules established by your business's organizational documents.

Finally, you'll notice that you'll only pay yourself an actual salary if you're a corporate shareholder who also works within the business as an executive, officer, or other employee.

Entity Type	How You Take Money	Self-Employment Tax
Sole Proprietor	Draw	Yes
Single-Member LLC	Draw	Yes
Partner	Distributive Share	Yes
Multi-Member LLC	Distributive Share	Yes
S Corp Shareholder	Distributive Share	Yes
C Corp Shareholder	Dividends	No
Corporate Executive/Employee	Salary	No

Keep in mind that no matter how you pay yourself, you must pay it from your profits, not your revenues. Remember that your profit is your revenue minus your expenses. In other words, you need to pay your expenses first in order to see how much is really left over for draws or distributions. For example, if you're paying yourself a large distribution or salary even though the business can't afford to make regular payments on its business loan, then you're going to seriously jeopardize your corporate-veil protection. If the loan company ever comes knocking, looking for its money, it's not going to look good that you were paying yourself and your other members a large share while you failed to make minimum payments to your creditors. The point, then, is to be realistic about your distributions and use your balance sheets and P&L statements to determine what is reasonable and what the business can afford.

Compensating Directors

Another important corporate decision is whether or not to compensate your directors. In years past, directors weren't paid salaries because they're usually shareholders as well; which means that they already receive dividends. In more recent years, though, it's become commonplace to pay directors regular salaries, aside from their shareholder dividends, as compensation for the more active role they play within the company. Keep in mind, though, that small businesses, in particular, don't usually pay their directors right away. Payments, however, may be authorized later, as your corporation becomes more stable and profitable. Paying your directors, of course, can affect your corporate veil, particularly if you don't follow proper procedures.

Your board of directors may receive payment for their services in one of three ways:

First, your articles of incorporation may actually provide a set salary for your directors. Be warned, though, that you should only do this if you're sure that the business will be profitable enough to cover it. This is also an option, however, if your corporation will be closely held and the shareholders, directors, and officers will all be one and the same. In that case, setting a director salary within your articles may actually be reasonable.

Second, your board of directors can vote to give themselves salaries. However, this can only happen if your bylaws or articles specifically give them permission to do so. This is a good option if your small business will need time to become profitable (as most do) but you want to have the option to pay your directors later on.

Finally, your shareholders can give your board the authority to establish director salaries. This means that your shareholders would hold a vote to determine if the board should receive salaries. If the shareholders vote yes, your board would then be able to vote to establish the director salaries.

If and when your board votes to set director salaries, keep in mind that no director should vote on his own salary. Let's say that you have five other shareholders besides yourself, and four of you also serve on the board of directors. After a year in business, the board has collectively decided to start awarding director salaries, through authority of the bylaws. You've determined that each director should receive a salary equal to the amount of work she performs for the business. So if you serve as the CEO, the other three board members would vote on your particular salary, but you should refrain from taking part in that vote. As a matter of record, this will make it very clear that you didn't just award yourself a salary, and that proper meeting and voting procedures were used.

The overall financial health of your corporation should be considered during this process. If your business is struggling to make a profit, it's probably not an ideal time to start paying your directors salaries or giving them sizeable raises. This is another surefire way to risk your corporate veil. If, for whatever reason, you're sued or audited, and your directors are making $90,000-a-year salaries, for example, while your loan payments are routinely being paid late, then the courts are likely to strip your corporate veil to find out why you're getting paid but the creditors aren't.

Bookkeeping and Accounting Wrap-up

For many of you, bookkeeping and accounting will be your least favorite part of running a business. If you're one of those exceptional souls who just loves math and numbers, then you should count yourself so lucky. If accounting isn't your thing, though, don't be dismayed. It's not a death sentence for your small business dreams and aspirations. There are countless tools available to help you with this process, and professionals abound to assist you with the really tricky stuff. If ever there was a time to solicit help in order to protect your corporate veil, bookkeeping and accounting is it. But at least you now have a basic understanding of what should happen and how it should look.

12

Funding and Borrowing

You have to spend money to make money. That's incredibly clichéd but it's true. If you're not willing to spend some money, your business is never going to launch, let alone grow.

Funding isn't *just* about staying afloat, though. If I've taught you anything through this journey it's that your corporate veil is tied up in nearly every single aspect of your business; and that includes how you finance it. Where your funding comes from and how you apply it to your small business can—you guessed it—either shelter or threaten your corporate-veil protection.

Initial Financing

Securing start-up costs is one of the most important aspects of starting a small business. Aside from the obvious fact that you need the money, it's also a critical opportunity to protect your corporate veil and create a solid foundation of compliance. Here, I'll briefly discuss some of the most common and accessible options for funding a new business venture and how they may affect your corporate veil. Just as with accounting and bookkeeping, my goal here is not to make you an expert, but simply to help you understand how funding your business can leave a personal liability trail straight to you.

Personal Resources

Nobody wants to launch a business with excessive debt and financial obligations to others, especially if the business operations are small. If you can finance your venture using your own resources and funds, then you'll have one less payment to worry about as you try to get your business off the ground. Here are a few conventional means for personally financing a small start-up:

Keep Your Day Job—Many small business owners launch while they still hold down day jobs. Having a steady source of income can provide some security, as well as funding, while you get your idea off the ground. This is a great option for sole proprietors and partnerships, although some corporate owners have done the same.

Personal and Retirement Savings—If you've managed to create a small nest egg for yourself, you may be able to tap into it for start-up costs. Personal savings accounts are much easier to access than retirement plans. Just be reasonable about how much you take. If you've contributed to a 401(k) or something similar, check the terms and conditions, as well as state laws, to determine whether or not you're allowed to use that money for a business purpose. Again, these are great options for a sole proprietor or partnership. Many LLCs and corporations have also gotten their starts from personal savings plans.

How they affect your corporate veil: The most important thing to understand when tapping into your own funds is that it's considered an investment and there is no corporate veil. That means that if your business fails, you're going to lose the money you put into it. It won't come back to you and there's nobody to back it up. The advantage, though, is that you won't be financially liable to anybody but yourself (at least for the start-up costs) if the business fails or falls on hard times.

Home Equity—If you're a proud homeowner and have equity in your home, you may be able to access it and use it to fund a start-up. There are two ways to access that equity. First, you can apply for a new mortgage that's larger than what you still owe, and then use the excess. Or you can apply for a line of credit. Simply put, a line of credit is money that's available to you when you need it, so you only make payments if you actually use it. The line of credit is usually equal to the amount of equity in your home because the bank will use your equity as collateral.

How it affects your corporate veil: Just like using other personal funds, using your home equity puts the full financial burden squarely on you. If you take out a second mortgage or use a home equity line of credit, the bank won't care that your business failed or didn't make a profit last month. Either way, you'll still owe them a payment. In other words, when you fund your business with equity from your personal residence, it will be considered an investment, complete with all of the risks.

Credit and Loans

Launching on our own dime isn't always an option. Sometimes we need more than we personally have to give or we simply don't have anything to start with at all. In that case, using credit and loans isn't always a bad thing. The key is to borrow wisely and document everything meticulously.

Credit Cards—Credit cards can be a curse or a blessing, depending on how you use them. As a start-up fund, credit cards should only be used to purchase equipment, furniture, or supplies. I generally caution against using a credit card to pay rent or make a deposit on office space. Credit cards should typically only be used for one-time purchases and to help establish your business credit.

Bank Loans—Banks are an obvious choice if you're looking for a loan. If you're looking for a business loan, though, your business plan is going to be a necessity. In Chapter 8, we discussed the importance of a business plan to help your business stay on track, meet goals, and stay organized. But it's also an invaluable tool when you're pitching to bankers and convincing them that your business is going to be viable. Some banks are hesitant to loan money to start-ups, but a well-researched business plan can nudge them in the right direction.

How they affect your corporate veil: Using credit and loans can come with some risk to your corporate veil. First, if you're operating an LLC or corporation, you should get the credit card in your business's name. This will make it very clear that the business is responsible for the payments and not you, as an individual. Loans are much the same way. If you can get the loan in your business's name, then it will take some of the liability off your shoulders; at least, in a legal sense.

However, this isn't always possible. Start-up business owners often have to put their personal signatures on business loans until the businesses obtain their own credit. If that's the case, understand that you'll be personally responsible for the payments, even if the business fails or struggles. Often what's required is a promissory note, which is literally just a promise to pay. The bank will keep the original and you should keep a copy for your records.

When you pay off the last of the loan, the original will be marked "Paid in Full" (or something similar) and returned to you. Keep this for your records in case there is ever a dispute about whether or not the loan was paid off.

If you're launching a business with other investors (discussed in just a moment) you'll want to discuss the possibility of having all of the members, partners, or initial shareholders listed on the loan or credit card as well. This spreads the risk, takes sole responsibility off your shoulders, and further solidifies the partnership.

Most importantly, if you use credit or loans, you need to keep careful records of how you spend the money. If you take out a business loan, for example, and use it to finish your basement, you'd better be able to prove that it served a business purpose. Did you finish the basement to create a dedicated home office, or did you make a personal gym? And when it comes to using the business credit card, make sure it's being used for business only! You may think it's harmless to use it to buy your daughter's birthday present (just this once), but that can seriously jeopardize your corporate-veil protection. Remember, any time you blur the line between you and your business, you're risking that veil. Make sure that your business funds and personal funds are clearly separated. And use those business loans and credit cards strictly for business purchases.

Family and Friends—If you opt to borrow from family and friends, you wouldn't be the first. Fathers have given money, mothers have pitched in for expenses, and friends have loaned money to a buddy with a dream. These types of personal loans can often be beneficial. They usually come with lower interest rates than banks, and it can be easier to convince your uncle that you'll be a success than it is to convince a banker. Just be sure that you're not accepting money from a family member who can't really afford it or one who doesn't understand the inherent risks of small business.

How it affects your corporate veil: When it comes to borrowing from family and friends, the risks are a bit more personal. While you won't be on the hook to a bank or commercial lender, you will be risking an important relationship. Many friendships have ended and families been destroyed over business ventures. If you're going to borrow from family or friends, be sure to put everything in writing and separate personal feelings from business matters as much as possible. In other words, treat it like any other business transaction. Draw up a contract, review it, make sure everybody involved is happy with it, and sign it as you would any other binding agreement. This will help to prevent misunderstandings and create established and agreed-upon rules for how the loan will be repaid and handled. Understand, of course, that you'll be personally liable for the repayment of the loan, unless the contract states otherwise.

Equity Investors

If you're launching a limited partnership, LLC, or corporation, you have an advantageous financing option: co-owners. These are the partners, members, and shareholders who invest right along beside you. These folks are known as "equity investors" because they're buying a piece of your business in return for some of the equity. Because they're *investing*, not lending, you don't have to guarantee that they'll get their money back. And, if you're operating as a formally filed entity, they'll receive corporate-veil protection just like you.

Your equity investors will play various roles within your business, depending on your entity type and what type of relationship you establish. Let's say that your recently widowed godmother wants to invest some of her inheritance in your woodworking business. So you establish the business as an LLC and set it up as manager-managed. You list your godmother as a member, but you take on the role of manager. You, then, manage the day-to-day operations while your godmother serves as a member, only helping to make big decisions about the LLC's general direction. You establish in your operating agreement that your godmother will receive 30 percent, for example, of all quarterly profits, so that she's guaranteed some kind of return on her investment, without you, personally, having to pay her back.

Or let's say that your college roommate wants to go all in with you. You establish a corporation, both investing a substantial amount of personal funds. You become the initial shareholders, and both decide to actively serve in the business as directors and officers. This would make your college roommate a more active equity investor, but an investor nonetheless. He'll have corporate-veil protection and responsibility for the operations of the business.

How they affect your corporate veil: These are just two of the countless ways that you might work with your equity investors. The point is that your investors are just that: they take a risk with you but they also receive some corporate-veil protection in return. Keep in mind what you have learned in previous chapters, though. Depending on what type of entity you form, your co-investors' transgressions may or may not jeopardize your personal corporate veil. If a shareholder in your corporation, for example, violates his duties of loyalty and care, it won't necessarily affect you and the other shareholders. As long as you have kept careful records and meeting minutes, you should be able to prove that the shareholder acted alone, leaving your corporate veil intact and leaving him responsible for his own choices. A partnership, on the other hand, lacks corporate-veil protection. So your partner's debts become your debts, and your contractual obligations become his contractual obligations. Bear this in mind when you join forces with other equity investors and decide which type of entity to form.

Document, Document, Document

Regardless how you fund your start-up, the name of the game is documentation. You should keep careful records of where your money comes from, how it's spent, and how and when it gets paid back. This will become especially important if you're ever audited. The IRS will want to see exactly where your money comes from and how it's being spent. If you can show that your business loans and credit cards are being used solely for business purchases, it's going to go a long way toward protecting your corporate veil. Similarly, if you can prove that you've been making regular payments to your lenders, using profits from the business, it will provide proof that your business is operating as a business and paying off its own debts.

Just like your meeting minutes, bylaws, and partnership agreements, credit card receipts and loan payment documentation will be vital to your corporate veil.

Borrowing Throughout

Once your business is established and the start-up phase is behind you, it will still need funds to keep going. Eventually, of course, the goal is for your business to be profitable enough to support itself. But that doesn't address the reality that the small business world comes with financial highs and lows. Factors like the economy, social issues, and personal choices and challenges can all affect your business's bottom line at any given time. Sometimes your business will experience smooth sailing. Other times, you may struggle to keep your head above water. While these valleys and peaks are not a given, they're a pretty typical part of small business life. Odds are you'll eventually experience both.

Sole proprietors and partners can borrow throughout the life of their businesses in much the same way that they fund it initially: credit cards, personal resources, and loans are all options. But corporations and LLCs have additional possibilities (and more rules, of course) that may not be obvious or readily understood. Here, we'll focus on those.

Secured Loans

Because corporations and LLCs are their own entities, they have the ability to accrue their own debts. This means that once your business is somewhat established, it will be able to borrow money without a personal promissory note from you. Usually, this requires the business to pledge property. In other words, since a human being isn't promising to pay back the loan, the business has to promise the bank something valuable, such as property, equipment, or accounts receivable. This is known as a secured loan and it creates a contractual obligation between the lender and the business entity, separate and apart from you.

If you operate a corporation, your board of directors will have the ability to obtain loans on behalf of the business without the shareholders' approval. The key, of course, is for the directors to use common sense and discretion. If the loan is used to pay the directors bigger salaries, then the shareholders may have a legitimate grievance.

If the loan is used to purchase equipment for a new product line, however, then that's a different story. Review Chapter 6 on corporations if you need a refresher on who has the power to make decisions within a corporation.

LLCs can usually obtain secured loans with the approval of the members. See Chapter 7 if you need a reminder of how power is distributed between members and managers.

Keep in mind that a business may be able to accrue its own debts, but a business can't sign its own name. We discussed in Chapter 9 the importance of getting the right person to sign, and this is especially true when it comes to securing financing and loans. If you're signing loan papers on behalf of your business, make sure that your signature block clearly shows that you are signing as the president, manager, CEO, or whatever title is accurate and relevant. In other words, make sure that whoever is actually signing for the loan is signing *on behalf of* the business and that she actually has the authority to do so. If not, whoever is signing may very well find herself personally responsible for the loan.

How they affect your corporate veil: Secured loans will protect the integrity of your corporate veil so long as you follow the rules. First, this means that your personal property can't be used to secure the loan. It must be property that's owned and held by the business itself. Second, the loan funds should always be used for a valid business purpose, and loan payments must be paid promptly and as agreed. Third, make sure that the right person signs! Finally, you must abide by your state laws, articles of incorporation, bylaws, and/or operating agreement. If you fail to follow any of these rules, you'll risk your corporate-veil protection.

Borrowing from Investors and Officers

Another option for corporations and LLCs is to borrow from the members, shareholders, directors, or officers.

This can be tricky, though, and should be handled with care and attention to detail.

First, always check your state statutes to make sure that there isn't some law prohibiting your business from borrowing money from insiders. Some states won't allow it, or only allow it under specific circumstances. Second, make sure that you abide by your articles of incorporation, bylaws, and/or operating agreement.

Some corporations and LLCs prohibit this practice in their organizational documents. This is especially true of larger businesses. Small businesses, however, are inclined to leave this as an option, particularly because they tend to be more closely held. This is a decision that you'll have to make when you're creating your business entity.

Your shareholders, directors, members, and officers can provide financing to your business in one of two ways: they can either lend the business money or they can lend the business credit. The key is to treat this transaction the same way you would a loan from a third party, like a bank. The loan should be well documented, preferably secured, and signed by the correct parties. Let's say that your LLC is ready to launch services in connection to its successful product line. The business needs some cash to fund a marketing campaign for the new services being offered. Rather than taking out a bank loan, one of your fellow members has offered to loan the business money from the recent sale of his personal home. The member would become the lender and the business should secure the loan. This can be done by promising that particular member a larger share of the profits or, perhaps, equipment owned by the business. Either way, it needs to look and operate as a legitimate loan, otherwise it will be treated as an investment. And an investment, remember, is not guaranteed to be returned.

The benefit of borrowing from an insider is that the insider is already personally invested in the business, so he'll likely be willing to give the business a lower interest rate and a more flexible payoff schedule. And this includes you. If, at any point in time, your business needs to be infused with some cash, you can personally loan your business the money. Always be sure to treat it like a loan and not an investment, though.

The Most Significant Risk

As we wrap up this chapter, keep in mind that borrowing and funding is a subject all its own. There is much more to it than I could possibly cover here. For our purposes, though, I want you to understand that how you borrow and fund your small business will make a difference to your corporate veil.

The most significant financial risk inherent to starting and running a business is potentially finding yourself personally liable if the business is sued or gets audited. Before you borrow or use any type of credit, do your research. Make sure that it's legal, that you're following your own organizational rules, and that the correct person is signing on behalf of the business. Always be critical of how your business funds are being spent and meticulously document and record every penny you borrow, earn, and spend. All of this will go a long way toward protecting your corporate veil and keeping your business in business.

13

Taxes and Deductions:
An Overview of Everybody's
Favorite Subject

I probably don't need to tell you (but it's worth repeating) that you don't want to mess with the IRS. That's
like poking a bear. No good can come of it. So as we come
to a close on our time here, my final message is on the
importance of taxes to your corporate veil. In this book, I
will give the big picture. For a more in-depth analysis and
tax-wise strategies, you will want to refer *Tax-Wise Business Ownership*, written by my partner Toby Mathis.

I mentioned in chapter 1 that lawsuits aren't the
only possible reason for a corporate veil to be pierced. If
you *or* your business is ever audited, the tax returns and
practices for both will be inspected by the IRS. If your
business hasn't paid its taxes properly, if your accounting procedures don't look right, or if your personal
returns show questionable income from your business,
then all bets will be off. The IRS is going to dig, scrutinize all of your financial and tax statements, and then

decide whether your taxes and finances were in compliance with all applicable laws. Remember, they'll also be looking for any evidence of fraud, and intent doesn't necessarily have to be a factor.

The point is not to scare you but to emphasize the importance of at least having a baseline understanding of how business taxes work and why they matter so much. Just as in the last two chapters, I'm not here to make you a small business tax expert. I just want you to understand basic taxation and deduction issues, and to appreciate the connection they have to your corporate-veil protection. This will help you to make more sensible and informed decisions as you move forward.

State Taxes

We're going to keep things simple to start.

First, just like you, your business will have to pay both state and federal taxes. Per the norm, state taxes vary widely, so I can't give you all those details here. It's important that you review your state tax laws *as* you're creating your business. If you wait until you're filing your first business tax return, you may very well discover that you've missed out on something important or overlooked a tax rule that would have saved you a substantial amount of money. So make this a priority as soon as you decide what type of entity to form.

In fact, it may even be a critical part of your decision-making process. For example, your state may have favorable tax laws for single-member LLCs, making it worth your while to form one of these, rather than operate as a sole proprietor. You'd want to know this from the beginning, wouldn't you?

Federal Taxes

Federal laws are more universal, apply to everybody, and come in three main categories:

1. Employment/Payroll

2. Income

3. Self-employment

Employment/Payroll Tax

Employment taxes are a fun bunch and can get a little complicated—but it's nothing we can't handle. As their name implies, these taxes will only be relevant if you have employees. *But* I would suggest reading this section regardless, because some of the information will overlap with, and even apply to, taxes for sole proprietors and corporations that don't have employees. In other words, its valuable information and worth the quick read!

First, we have the **federal income tax**. If you've ever been an employee (and most of us have), you'll recognize this tax. This is the tax that all employees in the U.S. pay. The money goes to fund things like police and fire departments, public schools, and public projects. If your small business has employees, it will be your responsibility to withhold income taxes from your employees' paychecks.

Every time you hire an employee, he'll need to complete a W-4 to choose his withholding status and state how many dependents he has. Based on that information, you'll withhold a certain amount of money from each of his paychecks. (We'll discuss how to determine the correct amount in just a moment.) The withdrawn funds should then be transferred to a trust account so that you can make recurring payments to the IRS.

Federal income tax rates vary depending on how high the income is, how many dependents the employee has, and whether he's single or married. In other words, the amount of money you withhold from each employee's paycheck depends on a lot of different factors.

In order to calculate how much you should withhold from each employee's paycheck, you'll have to refer to a document known as *IRS Publication 15-A*, which can easily be found on the IRS.gov website. This yearly publication uses a table to show you exactly how much you should be withholding.

Next, we have the Federal Insurance Contributions Act (FICA) which consists of Old Age, Survivors and Disability Insurance (OASDI) also known as **Social Security tax** and Hospital Insurance (HI) also known as **Medicare tax**. As the employer, it will also be your responsibility to withhold Social Security and Medicare taxes from your employees' paychecks. Social Security taxes are calculated based on a flat percentage, meaning that everybody pays the same rate. For example, the 2018 Social Security tax rate was 6.2 percent and the Medicare tax was 1.45 percent. So 6.2 percent plus 1.45 percent of each of your employees' paychecks would need to be withheld, in addition to the federal income tax withholding. Again, the funds should be held in trust and submitted in regular payments to the IRS. Be aware that the Social Security tax withholding percentage rates change annually, so make sure you check the new rates at the end of each calendar year. It's also important to note that, as the employer, you'll also have to pay a portion of the Social Security and Medicare taxes. In other words, the IRS expects half from the employee and half from the business itself.

Finally, we have the **federal unemployment tax**. This tax won't come out of your employees' pay at all. The unemployment tax is paid on your dime; or, to be more exact, your business's dime. The federal unemployment tax is also based on a flat percentage. The 2020 rate was 6 percent. So for every employee, you would have had to pay 6 percent of each employee's first $7,000 in earnings. For example, if you had five employees who each earned more than $7,000 from your business, you would have owed $420 in unemployment tax for each, totaling $2,100 for the year. This money, just like the Social Security and federal income tax withholdings, would have to be held and deposited periodically.

Before we move on to the self-employment and income taxes, I have one *huge* warning for you. **Never** borrow from your tax trust accounts. As tempting as it may be to dip into the account, it could be absolutely devastating to your corporate-veil protection.

Once you withhold that money from your employees' paychecks, it legally belongs to the IRS. It's not yours. It's not your business's. It belongs to Uncle Sam and "borrowing" it is essentially the same as stealing it. And there's very little help for you if you steal from Uncle Sam.

Income Tax

As a small business owner, there's no employer to withhold your income taxes for you. You'll have to calculate and pay them yourself. How you pay income taxes, though, will depend on which type of entity you operate as.

If you operate as a C Corporation, the corporation will have to report its own profits, losses, and business income to the IRS. Remember, the corporation is its own entity. Keep in mind, though, that many small, closely held corporations pay most of their profits to their shareholders (that's you) in the form of both dividends and salaries. When your corporation pays your salary, it's tax deductible by the corporation. In other words, it's possible for your corporation to have zero taxable income if it passes all of its profits on to you and your other shareholders and employees. This isn't always the case, though. If your business is going to grow, it needs to keep some of the profits and reinvest them back into the business's operations, inventory, facilities, etc. Your corporation will owe its own income taxes on whatever income, or profit, it has earned *and not paid out* by the end of the year.

Let's say that you own Writer's Glen, Inc., which is a small publishing company formed as a C Corporation. It's held by only you and your two adult children. Writer's Glen made a $150,000 profit last year, *after* you and your children were paid salaries for your work within the business and after deductions and expenses were subtracted. So the corporation would owe income taxes on $150,000 worth of income.

If you operate an LLC, your income taxes will depend on how you chose to have the business taxed. Remember that an SMLLC can choose to be taxed as a sole proprietor, while an LLC with multiple members can choose to be taxed as either a partnership or a corporation.

On the other hand, if you operate as a sole proprietor, partnership, SMLLC, or S Corporation your business taxes will flow through to your personal tax returns, as we've discussed more than once. (See how this is all connected?) This means that the business, itself, will not pay income taxes. *You* will pay the businesses income taxes on your personal return, based on how much of the business's income flowed to you. Let's say that you operate a partnership with your brother. The business's profits and losses are split evenly between the two of you. Last year, the partnership earned $100,000, so $50,000 will flow to you and $50,000 will flow to your brother. After subtracting expenses and deductions, the total income for the partnership ends up being $85,000. You would have to pay income taxes for $42,500 on your personal tax return and your brother would pay income taxes on the other $42,500 on his personal return.

Then, of course, you would still have to pay self-employment taxes for yourself.

Self-Employment Tax

Self-employment tax is the equivalent of the Social Security and Medicare taxes that are withheld from employees. In other words, just because you're self-employed doesn't mean that you're not expected to contribute to the pot.

Self-employment taxes, then, are based on a flat percentage rate that typically changes annually. The self-employment tax rate is generally much higher than the Social Security tax rates. That's because the IRS considers you both the employee and the employer, so they're going to charge you for both roles. Your self-employment taxes will be based on the income the business made, not you. In other words, your income from the business may be different than the business's income if you've reinvested some of the business profits back into the business. Self-employment taxes are based on the business's portion, not yours.

For example, if the net earnings of your single-member LLC (SMLLC) are $50,000 but you only paid yourself $35,000, the self-employment tax would be paid on the $50,000, not the $35,000.

IRS Publications

Thankfully, the IRS provides several free resources to help you navigate business tax matters. The *Circular E Employer's Tax Guide* is published yearly and is available on the IRS.gov website. It's chock-full of details on how to calculate income tax withholdings, which forms to use, etc. *IRS Publication 509 Tax Calendars* are also quite useful and will tell you when to file your business returns and when to make your payments and/or deposits for the taxes you withhold from your employees. Even if you plan on hiring a bookkeeper or accountant, I still highly recommend that you familiarize yourself with these forms. No matter how much help you have, at the end of the day, this is *your* small business. The more you know about what's going on, the more you can protect yourself, your investments, and your corporate veil.

Taxes and Your Corporate Veil

As you can probably imagine, there's a whole lot more to business taxes than we've just covered, but here's what you really need to understand: if you fail to withhold and pay the appropriate taxes, the IRS *will* come looking for its money. It won't be a matter of if, but when. Every day, the IRS team is hard at work inspecting returns and payments, and making sure that business owners and individuals alike are paying exactly what the law requires. I'm not telling you to tiptoe through your business taxes and finances. What I am telling you, though, is to make sure that it's all done right. If that means hiring a professional, then so be it. It will be well worth the investment to ensure that your corporate veil is protected from the unforgiving nature of the IRS.

Business Deductions

The IRS does give some grace in the form of business deductions. You've probably heard the term before but many don't know what it actually means. A "deduction" simply means that an item or expense can be deducted, or subtracted, from your business's annual income. For tax purposes, this reduces your business income, which, in turn, reduces the amount that your business will be taxed.

Look at it this way: If your business earned $185,000 last year, the LLC would owe income and Social Security taxes based on that amount. *But* if you subtracted the cost of your office lease, cell-phone plan, marketing expenses, legal and accounting expenses, and business-related travel costs, your taxable income might actually be more like $125,000.

This is known as the taxable income of the business and it can make a really big difference when it comes to how much you pay in taxes.

So (just to be clear) deductions are generally a good thing.

What counts as a legitimate deduction isn't always so clear, though. The IRS doesn't publish a master list of acceptable deductions. The general guideline is that a business can deduct expenses that are "Customary, Ordinary, Reasonable, and Necessary," which I abbreviate as "CORN." In other words, these are expenses that are legitimately related to your trade or profession and that were actually made in the pursuit of business. For example, if you're a real estate investor, you may purchase a digital camera so that you can take quality pictures of your properties for advertising purposes. This might actually count as a legitimate expense for your business so long as you only use the camera for business. But if you join the local gym and try to write it off as a business expense, the IRS probably isn't going to buy it, even if you claim that you're at the gym to find new clients. It's best to use common sense and honesty.

While not inclusive, the following is a list of commonly accepted business deductions:

▶ Legal, accounting, and other professional fees

- Yes, your attorney retainer and accounting costs may actually be tax deductible.

- ▶ Employee benefits and expenses
    - ◆ This includes wages, health plans, etc.

- ▶ Club and organization dues
    - ◆ Chamber of commerce membership dues? Yes. Country club dues? Probably not so much.

- ▶ Education and training expenses
    - ◆ Attending a seminar or webinar can be tax deductible.

- ▶ Software programs

- ▶ Books, magazines, and professional journals
    - ◆ *People* magazine doesn't count, but a journal dedicated to your profession probably does.

- ▶ Vehicle expenses
    - ◆ If you use your car for business travel, mileage may be deductible.

- ▶ Travel and meals
    - ◆ Did you travel out of state to secure a big new client? Your hotel stay may be deductible.

- ▶ Marketing and advertising
    - ◆ This one is pretty much a no-brainer.

Again, this is far from being an all-inclusive list. This is, however, a list of the most commonly deducted categories and expenses. Remember the general rule: customary, ordinary, reasonable, and necessary.

Also, bear in mind that business deductions are available to you no matter what type of entity you operate as. However, what's reasonable for a corporation might not be reasonable for a sole proprietor, and vice versa. You'll need to use your common sense (and morals) when deciding what to deduct.

The Hobby-Loss Rule

The Hobby-Loss Rule is important, especially for small business owners. Unless you're making fairly consistent income, there's a risk that the IRS might consider your venture more of a hobby than an actual business. If you're a freelance photographer, for example, and you only made a profit five of the last twenty-four months, the IRS might wonder if you're running a business or if you're just taking pictures for family and friends. It makes a really big difference when it comes to what you can deduct from your taxes.

To determine if your efforts are business or hobby, the IRS looks at nine key factors:

1. Does the time and effort you put into the activity indicate that you're trying to make a profit?

2. Do you behave in a businesslike manner? (Remember that?)

3. Do you know enough about the activity to successfully run a business doing it?

4. Has the activity made a profit at least three of the last five years?

5. Have you made a profit performing similar activities in previous years?

6. Do you anticipate a future profit on the appreciation of the assets? (In other words, will the equipment or supplies used for the activity be worth more in the future?)

7. Do you personally rely on the profits made through the activity?

8. Has the activity experienced losses? In other words, are you just spending money and not bringing any in?

9. Have you changed procedures or methods in an attempt to avoid losses and make more profits?

The IRS will look at all of these factors and circumstances if they're questioning the legitimacy of your business. And, just to be clear, the simple act of forming an entity doesn't convince the IRS that you're serious. You have to follow *all* of the compliance issues discussed throughout this book and make a genuine effort to create a profitable business.

2018 Tax Cuts and Jobs Act

Before we wrap this all up, I'm going to briefly discuss the *2018 Tax Cuts and Jobs Act*. It's the largest tax law passed in nearly three decades and it does have a meaningful impact on small business owners. It's an expansive piece of legislation, but we'll only focus on its impact on small business owners.

How you fare under the new tax laws will depend on several factors:

- ▸ Do you operate a pass-through entity?

- ▸ How much personal income do you receive from the business?

- ▸ How much Qualified Business Income (QBI) does the business make?

In other words, it depends.

Here are some of the provisions that will directly affect many businesses:

Section 179 and Bonus Depreciation

A business can now deduct up to $1 million of total qualified business equipment with a phase out of $2.5 million limited to the amount of income from the business activity. The act expanded the definition of the type of property to improvements to nonresidential property.

In addition, the new law increased the depreciation percentage under Section 168(k) from 50 percent to

100 percent in the year the qualified property was placed into service. This will be the case until 2022.

Interest Deduction

For business under $25 million, the deduction for business interest is now capped at 30 percent of the business's taxable income, with the additional amount being carried forward to future years. Businesses over $25 million and certain financial, real estate, and farming businesses are exempt from the limitation.

Net Operating Losses

Net operating losses are limited to 80 percent of the taxable income of the business.

Luxury Automobile Deduction

Business vehicles not claimed under the bonus depreciation now get a higher first year deduction of $10,000. This deduction is only calculated using actual business miles.

Entertainment Deduction

The ability to deduct entertainment expenses, including membership dues for clubs, is now disallowed by the new code.

Deductions for Meals

Meals provided for employees at the convenience of the employer and travel meals are now only 50 percent deductible.

Pass-Through Entities and Section 199A

The most notable advantage for owners of pass-through business entities (sole proprietors, SMLLCs, S Corporations, partnerships, etc.) is that you'll be able to automatically deduct 20 percent of your earnings before you have to calculate the amount of income tax you owe. That would mean that you could deduct $33,000 from your $165,000 annual income and only pay income taxes on the remaining $132,000. One important clause to note is that the standard deduction rate is 20 percent of qualified business income (QBI), as long as the total taxable income is less than $157,500 if single or $315,000 if married and filing jointly. Another note is that these amounts are adjusted annually by the IRS for inflation.

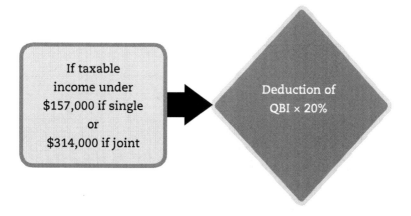

There are exceptions, rules, and variables of course, but the overall effect of the bill is a positive one for pass-through entity owners.

After $157,000 if single or $315,000 if married filing jointly, a phase-in reduction comes into play until taxable income levels reach $207,500 if single or $415,000 if filing jointly.

For incomes over $207,000 single/$415,000 MFJ, the formula becomes the lesser of QBI ´ 20% *or* the greater of 50% of W-2 wage limitation *or* W-2 wages ´ 25% + 2.5% of unadjusted basis on tangible property subject to depreciation. Whew! That was a lot, and we are not even done!

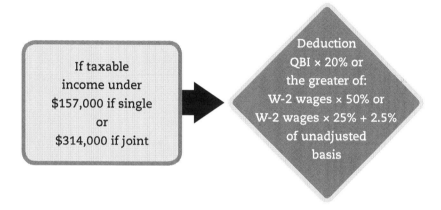

These same phase-out limits apply to service businesses such as attorneys, CPAs, medical professionals, performing arts, and the catch all, "any trade or business where the principal asset of such trade or business is the reputation or skill of one or more of its employees." However, after the taxpayer reaches $207,000 if single or $415,000 if filing jointly, then the tax payer loses all of the Section 199A deductions.

C Corporations

C Corps will see substantial benefits from the act. The highlight of the act, though, is the drastically reduced corporate tax rate. The corporate tax rate will drop from 35 percent to 21 percent. (The corporate tax is just the taxes that a C Corp pays on its income.) And 21 percent will be the lowest it's been since 1939!

Let's put that into numbers. Let's say that your C Corp had an income of $185,000 in 2018, after deductions, of course. The business would have had to pay approximately $64,750 in taxes. If your business earned the same $185,000 in 2018, it would only have to pay approximately $38,850 in corporate taxes. Clearly, that's a very big difference.

Per the norm, this new tax bill is far from being small, straightforward, simple, or perfect. Its exact impact on you and your small business will be based on multiple and varying factors. However, the standard deductions and drastically reduced corporate tax rate alone are enough to conclude that this act will likely have a positive effect on your business's bottom line and tax savings. In order to truly take advantage of the new tax structure and make sure that your corporate veil is protected and remains intact, it's highly recommended that you seek the advice and services of a tax professional.

14

Next Steps, Helpful Tips, and a Little Bit of Encouragement

So now what?

Well, now you act. Now that you know that your corporate veil is *everything*, you take meaningful steps toward protecting your future, your finances, your business, your family, and your life. Because, yes: all of these things are depending on the strength of your corporate veil.

Perhaps you've been operating a sole proprietorship and you picked up this book to find out how to take it to the next level. Or maybe you and a partner run a small shop that grew faster than expected. You may even have an established corporation already but you are concerned about lawsuits and audits. Some of you may just have great business concepts but absolutely no idea where to start with the legal logistics.

No matter where you are in the journey, the information found is this book still applies to you. Now is the time to strengthen that corporate veil, protect it like your life depends on it, and make it work for you!

Build a Solid Team

No man or woman is an island unto themselves, and this couldn't be truer than in business. Not only will you need good partners, responsible managers, and dependable employees, but you'll also need a team of trusted advisors.

I mentioned, more than once, the benefit of having a CPA on your side, and it's worth repeating one last time. An experienced CPA can be a lifesaver when it comes to maintaining your books and keeping accurate financial records. If you don't have one already, find one.

If your business is new or growing, there is no substitute for sound legal counsel—even if it's just a yearly checkup to make sure everything's still on track. If you don't have a good attorney, get one. It doesn't have to cost you a fortune, but the small upfront fees could save you tens of thousands of dollars in the future. Trust me (and the clients who wished they had met me sooner), it's worth every little penny!

And never underestimate the power of a good business coach and others to root you on. Build a support team around you and your business and know that their help is invaluable.

What Not To Do

Just as important as knowing what you should do next is knowing what *not* to do next.

First and foremost, do *not* put this book down and forget about it. Thousands of would-be entrepreneurs have read the great books, attended the awesome seminars, and listened attentively during the best webinars. And then they set their notes aside, where they sat and collected dust. What a disappointing and unfortunate waste of time. An opportunity squandered.

If you took the time to get this far, don't let it go to waste! Highlight it. Take notes. Keep it on your desk as a reference. Whatever you do, don't let your newfound knowledge grow idle, stale, and forgotten.

Second, never stop learning. The information in this book is vital and timely and key to running a small business effectively. But your business education should not end here. Besides following the specific steps laid out in the preceding thirteen chapters, you'll need more resources to refer to as your business grows, as new challenges arise, and as the laws and rules shift and change.

Access the Small Business Administration website, tap into the power of business networking groups, follow our blog, attend an event or webinar, or sign up to be a member. Even better, do all of the above. Small business ownership is a never-ending opportunity to learn and grow.

Enjoy the Ride

If there is one final piece of advice I could give you, it would be to enjoy the ride. Business is about promise, upward mobility, opportunities, and choice. We're privileged in this country to enjoy such freedoms, and the more we exercise them properly, the more they'll grow. And the more they grow, the more people you can help. And the more people you can help, the better off we'll all be.

So put in the hard work and follow the rules. Cross your T's and dot your I's to protect that corporate veil, but always, always enjoy the ride. If you appreciate your business and take care of it properly, the opportunities are endless. Lastly, I wish you the best of success not only in your business, but also your lives.

Appendix

Sample Meetings and Resolutions

199

Action by Incorporator of ABA Services, Inc. A Nevada Corporation

The undersigned, Michael P. Bowman, the sole incorporator of ABA Services, Inc., a Nevada corporation, resolves and directs that the following resolutions are recorded:

Approval of Articles of Incorporation.

> **RESOLVED:** that the Articles of Incorporation of this Corporation were effective as of the date filed in the office of the Secretary of State of Nevada, are approved by the incorporator.

Election of Directors.

> **RESOLVED:** that the following are unanimously elected as Directors of the Corporation, to serve until their successors are duly elected and shall have duly qualified:

John Doe
Jane Doe

These resolutions are approved as an action taken by the incorporator of this Corporation on the Sixth day of April, 2020.

INCORPORATOR

Michael P. Bowman

Action by Incorporator of ABA Services, Inc.

Minutes of the Organizational Meeting of the Board of Directors of ABA Services, Inc. A Nevada Corporation

The organizational meeting of the Board of Directors of ABA Services, Inc., a Nevada business corporation, was held on the Sixth day of April, 2020, at Las Vegas, Nevada, at 9:00 a.m.

The following Directors were present:

John Doe

Jane Doe

A sufficient number of Directors were present to constitute a quorum for the purposes of conducting the organizational meeting.

An election was held, and John Doe was appointed temporary Chairman and Jane Doe was appointed temporary Secretary, each to serve until the close of the meeting.

Approval and Ratification of the Articles of Incorporation

A motion was made and seconded to approve the Articles of Incorporation filed in the Office of the Secretary of State of Nevada. Following discussion, the motion was passed by majority vote, and it was:

RESOLVED: that the Articles of Incorporation of this Corporation, as filed in the Office of the Secretary of State of Nevada are approved.

Compensation of Directors

A motion was made and seconded and, following discussion, the motion was passed by majority vote, and it was:

RESOLVED: that the Directors will not receive compensation for service to the Corporation, but the Corporation will reimburse the Directors for their reasonable out-of-pocket expenses incurred in the performance of their duties as Directors.

FURTHER, it is RESOLVED that if cash-flow restraints prevent the reimbursement of the Directors, the reimbursement may be reduced or postponed and carried on the books for future payments.

Issuance of Stock

A motion was made and seconded and, following discussion, the motion was passed by unanimous vote, and it was:

RESOLVED, that in consideration of the payment, in cash, to or on behalf of, the Corporation, the sufficiency of which is hereby expressly acknowledged, the President and Secretary of the Corporation are hereby authorized and directed, upon receipt by, or by others on behalf of, the Corporation of such cash from the person specified below, to issue to such person a certificate or certificates representing the ownership by them of the number of shares of fully paid and non-assessable shares of common stock of the Corporation as is also set forth below opposite his name:

Shareholder	Shares	Type	Issued For	Voting/Non Voting
John Doe	500	Common	Cash	Voting
Jane Doe	500	Common	Cash	Voting

RESOLVED: that the form of stock certificate to evidence shares of common stock of the Corporation, which has been presented to and reviewed by each director of the Corporation, is hereby adopted as the form of stock certificate for the shares of common stock of the Corporation, a specimen thereof being attached hereto and incorporated by reference herein.

Election of Officers

The Chairman of the meeting then called for the election of Officers of the Corporation. A motion was made and seconded and, following discussion, the motion was passed by majority vote, and it was:

RESOLVED: that the following persons are elected as officers of the Corporation in the respective capacities identified after their names. Each person's term of office is until the first annual meeting of the Board of Directors and until their respective successors are elected and qualified.

John Doe	President and Treasurer
Jane Doe	Vice-President and Secretary

FURTHER, it is RESOLVED that the Corporation must reimburse the officers of the Corporation for their reasonable out-of-pocket expenses incurred in the performance of their duties as such officers.

Bylaws Enacted

The Secretary then presented a proposed set of bylaws for regulation and management of the Corporation. After review by the Directors, a motion was made and seconded and, following discussion, the motion was passed by majority vote, and it was:

RESOLVED: that the Bylaws attached to this instrument and incorporated by reference are declared the Bylaws of the Corporation and a copy of such bylaws is hereby directed to be inserted into the minute book of the Corporation and is incorporated by reference herein.

Resident Agent

A motion was made and seconded and, following discussion, the motion was passed by majority vote, and it was:

RESOLVED: that Anderson Registered Agents whose address is

3225 McLeod Drive, Suite 110
Las Vegas, Nevada 89121

is appointed Resident Agent of this Corporation and authorized to discharge the duties of Resident Agent.

RESOLVED: that the Secretary will supply the Resident Agent with a copy of the Corporation's Articles of

Incorporation, Bylaws, and stock ledger statement to be kept on file by the Resident Agent.

Business Address

A motion was made and seconded and, following discussion, the motion was passed by majority vote, and it was:

RESOLVED: that the business addresses of the corporation shall be

3225 McLeod Drive, Suite 100
Las Vegas, Nevada 89121

Reimbursement of Startup Costs

A motion was made and seconded and, following discussion, the motion was passed by majority vote, and it was:

RESOLVED: that the Treasurer of the Corporation be and hereby is authorized to pay all fees and expenses incident to, necessary, or arising out of the organization of the Corporation and to reimburse any person who has made any disbursement therefore.

Fiscal Year

A motion was made and seconded and, following discussion, the motion was passed by majority vote, and it was:

RESOLVED: that the fiscal year of the corporation shall end on the 31st day of March, and shall begin on 1st day of April in each year.

Actions Taken by Anderson Business Advisors

A motion was made and seconded and, following discussion, the motion was passed by unanimous vote, and it was:

> **RESOLVED:** that the actions taken by Anderson Business Advisors are hereby approved, ratified, and adopted as if done pursuant to corporate authorization.

Business Purpose

A motion was made and seconded and, following discussion, the motion was passed by unanimous vote, and it was:

> **RESOLVED:** that the Corporation is organized to provide centralized management of investments and business activities and to engage in all lawful business activity as may come before the Corporation.

> **RESOLVED:** that in order to accomplish the foregoing purposes, the Corporation may engage in any other activities, which are related or incidental to the foregoing purposes, as may be determined by the Corporation's Board of Directors.

> **RESOLVED:** that the proper officers of the Corporation are hereby authorized and directed to make and file such certificates, reports, or other instruments that may be required by law to be filed in any state to authorize the corporation to transact business in each state.

Preparation of Appropriate Corporate Books

A motion was made and seconded and, following discussion, the motion was passed by unanimous vote, and it was:

RESOLVED: that the proper officer of the Corporation will cause to be prepared appropriate books and records with respect to the capital stock of the Corporation, in which will be recorded, among other things, the names and addresses of the stockholders and the number of shares held by each.

Mileage Reimbursement

A motion was made and seconded and, following discussion, the motion was passed by unanimous vote, and it was:

RESOLVED: that the Treasurer of the Corporation will reimburse each Officer, Director, and employee of the Corporation at the then existing IRS published standard mileage rate for any use of a personal vehicle driven while conducting business for the Corporation.

Conducting Business

A motion was made and seconded and, following discussion, the motion was passed by majority vote, and it was:

RESOLVED: that for the purpose of authorizing the Corporation to do business in any state, territory or dependency of the United States or any foreign country in which it is necessary or expedient for this Corporation to transact business, the proper officers of this Corporation are hereby authorized to appoint and substitute all necessary agents or attorneys for service of process, to designate and change the location of all necessary statutory offices and, under the corporate seal, to make and file all necessary certificates, reports, powers of attorney, and other instruments as may be required by the laws of such state, territory, dependency, or country to authorize the corporation to transact business therein.

Small Business Corporation

A motion was made and seconded and, following discussion, the motion was passed by majority vote, and it was:

> **RESOLVED:** that the Corporation is a "small business corporation" as defined in the Internal Revenue Code and the regulations issued thereunder.

Section 1244

A motion was made and seconded and, following discussion, the motion was passed by majority vote, and it was:

> **RESOLVED:** that the Directors desire to qualify the Corporation's stock as Section 1244 stock;

> **RESOLVED:** that ABA Services, Inc., hereby adopts a plan to have its stock classified as Section 1244 stock and offered for sale as such;

> **RESOLVED:** that the maximum amount to be received by this Corporation in consideration for its stock to be issued pursuant to this plan shall not exceed One Million and no/100 Dollars ($1,000,000.00).

> **RESOLVED:** that the stock issued pursuant to this plan shall be issued only for money and other property, but excluding other stock or securities; and

RESOLVED: that the officers of this Corporation shall take such action as is necessary to carry this plan into effect and especially to keep such records as are required by the Internal Revenue Service.

Banking Resolution

A motion was made and seconded and, following discussion, the motion was passed by unanimous vote, and it was:

RESOLVED: that the President and Secretary are authorized from time to time to select one or more depository banks for the funds of this Corporation. The bank resolutions required by the depository or depositories are adopted by the Board of Directors. The Secretary is directed to cause a copy of the resolutions to be inserted into the minute book following this consent. The President and Secretary are authorized to sign all drafts, checks, and other instruments or orders for the payment on any corporate bank accounts without the check or instrument being countersigned by the other of them.

RESOLVED: that the Board of Directors hereby adopts the form resolution of said bank (as completed) which appears in the form which is attached hereto and incorporated by reference herein, and the appropriate officers of the Corporation are hereby authorized to certify such form resolution of said bank as having been adopted by this Corporation and to furnish copies of this resolution to the said bank upon its request.

Borrowing

A motion was made and seconded and, following discussion, the motion was passed by unanimous vote, and it was:

> **RESOLVED:** that only the duly elected officers of the Corporation, acting either singularly or jointly as directed from time to time by resolution of the directors, be authorized to borrow money for, on behalf of, and in the name of the Corporation, but only pursuant to specific authorization by resolution of the Board of Directors as may from time to time be adopted.

Payment of All Fees and Expenses to Incorporate

A motion was made and seconded and, following discussion, the motion was passed by unanimous vote, and it was:

> **RESOLVED:** that the Treasurer is authorized and directed to pay all fees and expenses incident to and necessary for the organization and qualification of the Corporation, including, without limitation, all legal and accounting fees and costs to procure proper corporate books.

Authorization to Establish Employee Benefit Plans

A motion was made and seconded and, following discussion, the motion was passed by unanimous vote, and it was:

> **RESOLVED:** that the officers of the Corporation are authorized to investigate and pursue establishing health insurance, medical reimbursement, life insurance, pension, profit sharing, or other plans for the benefit of Officers, Directors, and employees of the Corporation.

FURTHER, it is RESOLVED that, to the extent necessary or advisable, the President is authorized and directed to prepare and submit proposals to the Board of Directors for the adoption of any such plans.

Authorization to Establish Employee Wellness Plan

A motion was made and seconded and, following discussion, the motion was passed by unanimous vote, and it was:

RESOLVED: that the corporation adopt a wellness care plan to pay expenses for preventative health care costs, including, but not limited to, membership at a fitness or health club, vitamins, etc., for the benefit of officers, and directors, and employees of the Corporation.

Hiring of Employees

A motion was made and seconded and, following discussion, the motion was passed by majority vote, and it was:

RESOLVED: that the President of the Corporation is hereby authorized and directed to hire and employ such personnel and other workers as the President deems necessary for the effective operation of the Corporation's business; and that the President of the Corporation is hereby authorized to pay all employees and workers of the Corporation such salary, wage, and other compensation as the President shall deem appropriate from time to time; and that the President of the Corporation shall have full power and authority to conduct all aspects of day-to-day operations of the Corporation's business as the President deems justified and appropriate.

Ratification of Prior Actions

A motion was made and seconded and, following discussion, the motion was passed by unanimous vote, and it was:

> **RESOLVED:** that all actions taken or contracts entered into up to this time, as well as all actions taken or contracts entered into by any promoter, incorporator, or Director, as individuals acting for the Corporation, are approved by the Corporation. All contracts adopted as though the individual had at that time full power and authority to act for the Corporation are approved by the Corporation as if each and every act had been done under the specific authorization of the Corporation.

With no further business to conduct, the meeting was adjourned upon motion made and seconded and passed by majority vote.

DATED, this 6th day of April, 2020

_____

John Doe / Director

_____

Jane Doe / Director

Resolution of the Board of Directors to Open a Corporate Bank Account for ABA Services, Inc. A Nevada Corporation

The undersigned, being a majority or all of the members of the Board of Directors of ABA Services, Inc., a Nevada Corporation, having met and discussed the business herein set forth, have unanimously:

> **RESOLVED:** that the officers of ABA Services, Inc., are ordered to, in the name of this Corporation, open a bank account located in Nevada for the deposit of funds belonging to the Corporation.

> **RESOLVED:** that the authorized individual(s) of the Corporation shall be authorized to endorse checks, drafts, or other evidences of indebtedness made payable to the Corporation. All checks, drafts, and other instruments obligating the Corporation to pay money out of the bank account shall be signed on behalf of the Corporation by the following individuals:

John Doe	President and Treasurer
Jane Doe	Vice-President and Secretary

> **RESOLVED:** that the bank is authorized to honor and pay any and all checks and drafts of the Corporation signed by the individuals named in the preceding sentence and that said individuals are authorized to com-

plete and sign standard account authorization forms (provided that the forms do not vary materially from the terms of this resolution).

RESOLVED: that the Treasurer of the Corporation shall submit a copy of any completed account authorization forms to the Secretary of the Corporation, who shall attach the forms to this resolution and place them in the corporate records book.

DATED, this 6th day of April, 2020

_____

John Doe / Director

_____

Jane Doe / Director

Resolution of ABA Services, Inc., to
Open a Corporate Bank Account

Resolution of the Board of Directors to Issue Shares for ABA Services, Inc. A Nevada Corporation

The undersigned, being a majority or all of the members of the Board of Directors of ABA Services, Inc., a Nevada Corporation, do hereby consent in writing to the adoption of the following resolution:

RESOLVED: that the stock of the Corporation shall be issued to the named individual(s) below. The number or amount of shares shall be indicated, and what the shares were issued for, such as, cash, property, services performed, or other assets received and indicated. The type of shares and the voting or non-voting rights are also indicated below:

Shareholder	Shares	Type	Issued For	Voting/Non Voting
John Doe	500	Common	Cash	Voting
Jane Doe	500	Common	Cash	Voting

IN WITNESS THEREOF, the undersigned have executed this written consent as of the date hereof.

Dated this 6th day of April, 2020

_____

John Doe / Director

_____

Jane Doe / Director

Resolution of ABA Services, Inc. to Issue Shares

Resolution of the Board of Directors for Reimbursement of Medical Care Expenses for ABA Services, Inc. A Nevada Corporation

The Directors of the Corporation hereby authorize a Medical Care Reimbursement Plan for ABA Services, Inc., a Nevada Corporation.

1. Benefits

The Corporation shall reimburse all eligible employees or officers for expenses incurred by themselves and their dependents, as defined in IRC subsection 152, for medical care, as defined in IRC subsection 213, subject to the conditions and limitations as hereinafter set forth. It is the intention of the Corporation that the benefits payable to eligible employees or officers shall be excluded from their gross income pursuant to IRC subsection 105.

2. Limitations

The Corporation shall reimburse any eligible officer and/or employee in any fiscal year for all of their medical care expenses.

Reimbursement or payment provided under this Plan shall be made by the Corporation only in the event and to the extent that such reimbursement or payment is not provided under any insurance policy(ies), whether owned by the Corporation or the employee, or under any other health or accident or wage continuation plan. In the event that such insurance policy(ies) exists, providing for reimbursement in whole or in part, then to the extent of such coverage under the policy or plan, the Corporation shall be relieved of any and all liability hereunder.

3. Submission of Proof

Any officer and/or employee applying for reimbursement under this Plan shall submit, quarterly, to the Corporation all bills for medical care, including premium notices for accident or health insurance, for verification by the Corporation prior to payment. Failure to comply herewith, the Corporation, using its own discretion, may terminate such eligible officers' and/or employees' rights to said reimbursement.

4. Discontinuation

This Plan shall be subject to termination at any time by vote of the Board of Directors, however, the medical care expenses incurred prior to termination shall be reimbursed or paid in accordance with the terms of this plan.

5. Determination

The President shall determine all questions arising from the administration and interpretation of the Plan except where reimbursement is claimed by the President. In such case the Board of Directors shall decide.

DATED, this 6th day of April, 2020

_____

John Doe / Director

_____

Jane Doe / Director

Revolving Line of Credit Agreement

This Revolving Line of Credit Agreement (the "Agreement") is made and entered into in this 6th day of April, 2020, by and between ABA Services, Inc. (the "Borrower"), and John Doe and Jane Doe (the "Lender," whether one or more).

In consideration of the mutual covenants and agreements contained herein, the parties agree as follows:

Revolving Line of Credit. Subject to the terms and conditions contained herein and in the other documents, instruments, and agreements executed in connection with the Loan and the security therefor ("Loan Documents"), Lender will establish for Borrower the Loan as a revolving line of credit against which Lender will make advances ("Advances") from time to time for the purpose of providing working capital to Borrower. Subject to the terms hereof, Borrower shall have the right to obtain Advances, repay Advances, and obtain additional Advances; however, all the Advances hereunder shall be viewed as a single loan. At no time shall the unpaid principal balance of the Loan exceed One Hundred Fifty Thousand Dollars ($150,000.00) (the "Credit Limit").

Note. The Loan shall be evidenced by a promissory note ("Note") of even date herewith in a form prepared and approved by Lender in the Maximum Amount, payable in accordance with the terms thereof. Interest on the principal amount outstanding from time to time shall be charged as provided in the Note and should such rate of interest as calculated thereunder exceed that allowed by law, the applicable rate of interest will be the maximum rate of interest allowed by applicable law.

Security. The Note is unsecured.

Advances. Any request for an Advance may be made from time to time and in such amounts as Borrower may choose; provided, however, any requested Advance will not, when added to the outstanding principal balance of all previous Advances, exceed the Credit Limit. Requests for Advances may be made orally or in writing by such officer of Borrower authorized by it to request such Advances. Until such time as Lender may be notified otherwise, Borrower hereby authorizes its president or any vice president to request Advances. Lender may deposit or credit the amount of any requested Advance to Borrower's checking account with Lender. Lender may refuse to make any requested Advance if an event of default has occurred and is continuing hereunder either at the time the request is given or the date the Advance is to be made, or if an event has occurred or condition exists which, with the giving of notice or passing of time or both, would constitute an event of default hereunder as of such dates.

Term. The term of this Agreement is from the date of this Agreement through and including January 1, 2022 (the "Term"). The last day of the Term will be sometimes referred to below as the "Maturity Date."

Interest. All sums advanced pursuant to this Agreement shall bear annual interest from the date each Advance is made until paid in full at the Short Term AFR rate as published in the *Wall Street Journal* ("Effective Rate").

Manner of Calculation. Interest shall be calculated on the basis of a three hundred sixty (360) day year for actual days elapsed. Interest will be charged on the principal balance of the

Line of Credit Agreement

loan that remains outstanding from time to time.

Interest Limitation. Notwithstanding any other provision of this Agreement or of any instrument securing this Agreement or any other instrument executed in connection with the Loan evidenced hereby, it is expressly agreed that the amounts payable under this Agreement or under the other aforesaid instruments for the payment of interest or any other payment in the nature of or which would be considered as interest or other charge for the use or loan of money shall not exceed the highest rate allowed by law, from time to time, to be charged by Lender. In the event the provisions of this Agreement or of any instruments referred to in this paragraph, regarding the payment of interest or other payments in the nature of or which would be considered as interest or other charge for the use or loan of money, operate to produce a rate that exceeds such limitation, then the excess over such limitation will not be payable and the amount otherwise agreed to have been paid shall be reduced by the excess so that such limitation will not be exceeded, and if any payment actually made shall result in such limitation's being exceeded, the amount of the excess shall constitute and be treated as a payment on the principal hereof and shall operate to reduce such principal by the amount of such excess, or if in excess of the principal indebtedness, such excess shall be refunded.

Payments. Principal and interest shall be due and payable and shall be paid at 3225 McLeod Drive, Suite 100 Las Vegas, Nevada 89121, or at such other place as the Lender may designate from time to time as follows:

i. Payments. Accrued interest shall be payable upon refinancing of any proportion to be made from time to time as provided in the Loan Agreement being executed on or about the date hereof. Accrued interest shall be due and payable and shall be paid commencing on the sale of any property secured by this Agreement date that is exactly one (1) month following the date of this Agreement, and on the same day of each succeeding monthly period thereafter through and including the same day of the month next preceding the Maturity Date.

ii. Principal Reductions. Principal payments shall be made from time to time as provided in the Loan Agreement being executed on or about the date hereof.

iii. Maturity Date. On the Maturity Date, all indebtedness evidenced by this Agreement (whether unpaid principal, accrued interest, or otherwise) that remains unpaid shall be due and payable and shall be paid.

Prepayment. Borrower shall have the option of prepaying all or any part of the principal of this Agreement at any time during the term of this Agreement, without notice, premium, or penalty for the privilege of such prepayments. The Lender may require that any partial prepayments be made on the date payments are due. In the event of any full prepayment, all accrued interest and other charges evidenced by this Agreement and the instruments of security for this Agreement shall be paid at the same time as such full principal prepayments.

Consent and Waiver. Each Obligor (which term shall mean and include the Borrower, each guarantor, each endorser, and all others who may become liable for all or any part of the obligations evidenced and secured hereby), does hereby, jointly and severally: (a) consent to any forbearance or extension of the time or manner of payment hereof and to the release of all or any part of any security held by the Lender to secure payment of this Agreement and to the subordination of any instrument of security securing this Agreement as to all or any part of the property encumbered thereby, all without notice or consent of that party; (b) agree that no course of dealing or delay or omission or forbearance on the part of the Lender in exercising or enforcing any of its rights or remedies hereunder or under any instrument securing this Agreement shall impair or be prejudicial to any of the Lender's rights and remedies hereunder or to the enforcement hereof and that the Lender may extend or postpone the time and manner of payment and performance of this Agreement and any instrument securing this Agreement, may grant forbearances and may release, wholly or partially, any security held by the Lender as security for this Agreement and release, partially or wholly, any person or party primarily or secondarily liable with respect to this Agreement, all without notice to or consent by any party primarily or secondarily liable hereunder and without thereby releasing, discharging, or diminishing its rights and remedies against any other party primarily or secondarily liable hereunder; and (c) except as otherwise set forth in this Agreement and the instruments of security for this Agreement, waive notice of acceptance of this Agreement, notice of the occurrence of any default hereunder or under any instrument securing this Agreement, and presentment, demand, protest, notice of dishonor, and notice of protest, and notices of any and all action at any time taken or omitted by the Lender in connection with this Agreement or any instrument securing this Agreement, and waive all requirements necessary to hold that party to the liability of that party.

Events of Default. The happening of any of the following events shall constitute a default hereunder: (a) failure of any Obligor to pay any principal, interest, or any other sums required hereunder when due under this Agreement; or (b) a default shall occur in any instrument securing this Agreement or in any other instrument executed in connection with the Loan evidenced hereby, which is not cured within the applicable curative period set forth in such instruments; (c) a filing by Borrower of a voluntary petition in bankruptcy seeking reorganization, arrangement or readjustment of debts, or any other relief under the Bankruptcy Code as amended or under any other insolvency act or law, state or federal, now or hereafter existing; or (d) a filing of an involuntary petition against Borrower in bankruptcy seeking reorganization, arrangement or readjustment of debts, or any other relief under the Bankruptcy Code as amended, or under any other insolvency act or law, state or federal, now or hereafter existing, and the continuance thereof for sixty (60) days undismissed, unbonded, or undischarged.

Acceleration. If a default shall occur hereunder which is not cured within thirty (30) days, then at the option of the Lender, the entire principal sum then remaining unpaid and accrued interest shall immediately become due and payable without notice or demand, and said principal shall bear interest from such date at the highest legal rate permitted by law, from time to time, to be charged by Lender; it being agreed that interest not paid when due shall, at the option of the Lender, draw interest at the rate provided for in this paragraph. Failure to exercise the above options shall not constitute a waiver of the right to exercise the same in the event of any subsequent default.

Remedies. Upon the occurrence of an event of default as defined above, Lender may declare the entire unpaid principal balance, together with accrued interest thereon, to be immediately due and payable without presentment, demand, protest, or other notice of any kind. Lender may suspend or terminate any obligation it may have hereunder to make additional Advances. To the extent permitted by law, Borrower waives any rights to presentment, demand, protest, or notice of any kind in connection with this Agreement. No failure or delay on the part of Lender in exercising any right, power, or privilege hereunder will preclude any other or further exercise thereof or the exercise of any other right, power, or privilege. The rights and remedies provided herein are cumulative and not exclusive of any other rights.

Borrower. The Borrower warrants and represents to Lender that it is a Corporation duly formed, presently existing and in good standing under the laws of the State of Nevada.

Law. This Agreement is executed under seal and constitutes a contract under the laws of the State of Nevada, and shall be enforceable in a Court of competent jurisdiction in that State, regardless of in which jurisdiction this Agreement is being executed.

Headings. The headings of the paragraphs contained in this Agreement are for convenience of reference only and do not form a part hereof and in no way modify, interpret, or construe the meaning of the parties hereto.

THE UNDERSIGNED ACKNOWLEDGES THAT THE LOAN EVIDENCED HEREBY IS FOR COMMERCIAL PURPOSES ONLY AND NOT FOR PERSONAL, FAMILY, OR HOUSEHOLD PURPOSES.

EXECUTED on the day and year first written above.

Borrower

ABA Services, Inc.

By, John Doe as its President
Lender

John Doe

Jane Doe

Promissory Note

$150,000.00   6th day of April, 2020

This Promissory Note (the "Note") is made and executed as of the date referred to above, by and between ABA Services, Inc. (the "Borrower"), promises to pay to the order of John Doe and Jane Doe (the "Lender," whether one or more). By this Note, the Borrower promises and agrees to pay to the order of Lender, at 3225 McLeod Drive, Suite 100, Las Vegas, Nevada 89121 or at such other place as Lender may designate in writing, the principal sum of One Hundred Fifty Thousand Dollars ($150,000.00), or the aggregate unpaid principal amount of all advances made by Lender to Borrower pursuant to the terms of a Revolving Line of Credit Agreement (the "Loan Agreement") of even date herewith, whichever is less, together with interest thereon from the date each advance is made until paid in full, both before and after judgment, at the Short Term AFR rate as published in the *Wall Street Journal*.

Borrower shall pay accrued interest on the outstanding principal balance under the Note on an annual basis commencing on April 6, 2020 and continuing on the anniversary day of each year thereafter until paid in full. The entire unpaid principal balance, together with any accrued interest and other unpaid charges or fees hereunder, shall be due and payable on January 1, 2022 (the "Maturity Date").

Prepayment in whole or part may occur at any time hereunder without penalty; provided that the Lender shall be provided with not less than ten (10) days notice of the Borrower's intent to pre-pay; and provided further that any such partial prepayment shall not operate to postpone or suspend the obligation to make, and shall not have the effect of altering the time for payment of the remaining balance of the Note as provided for above, unless and until the entire obligation is paid in full. All payments received hereunder shall be applied, first, to any costs or expenses incurred by Lender in collecting such payment or to any other unpaid charges or expenses due hereunder; second, to accrued interest; and third, to principal.

An event of default will occur if any of the following events occurs: (a) failure to pay any principal or interest hereunder within ten (10) days after the same becomes due; (b) if any representation or warranty made by Borrower in the Loan Agreement or in connection with any borrowing or request for an advance thereunder, or in any certificate, financial statement, or other statement furnished by Borrower to Lender is untrue in any material respect at the time when made; (c) default by Borrower in the observance or performance of any other covenant or agreement contained in the Loan Agreement; (d) filing by Borrower of a voluntary petition in bankruptcy seeking reorganization, arrangement or readjustment of debts, or any other relief under the Bankruptcy Code as amended or under any other insolvency act or law, state or federal, now or hereafter existing; or (e) filing of an involuntary petition against Borrower in bankruptcy seeking reorganization, arrangement or readjustment of debts, or any other relief under the Bankruptcy Code as amended, or under any other insolvency act or law, state or federal, now or hereafter existing, and the continuance thereof for sixty (60) days undismissed, unbonded, or undischarged.

Any notice or demand to be given to the parties hereunder shall be deemed to have been given to and received by them and shall be effective when personally delivered or when deposited in the U.S. mail, certified or registered mail, return receipt requested, postage prepaid, and addressed to the party at his or its last known address, or at such other address as the one of the parties may hereafter designate in writing to the other party.

The Borrower hereof waives presentment for payment, protest, demand, notice of protest, notice of dishonor, and notice of nonpayment, and expressly agrees that this Note, or any payment hereunder, may be extended from time to time by the Lender without in any way affecting its liability hereunder.

In the event any payment under this Note is not made at the time and in the manner required, the Borrower agrees to pay any and all costs and expenses which may be incurred by the Lender hereof in connection with the enforcement of any of its rights under this Note or under any such other instrument, including court costs and reasonable attorneys' fees. This Note shall be governed by and construed and enforced in accordance with the laws of Nevada.

EXECUTED on the day and year first written above.

ABA Services, Inc.

_____

By, John Doe as its President

Authorize Borrowing on Line of Credit for ABA Services, Inc. A Nevada Corporation

WHEREAS, this Company desires to borrow money, be it

RESOLVED, that the proper officers of this Company are hereby authorized to borrow from John Doe and Jane Doe ("Lender") for and on behalf of this Company, a sum not to exceed One Hundred Fifty Thousand Dollars ($150,000.00), on its promissory note maturing five (5) years from the date hereof, to be signed by the proper officers of this Company, and to bear interest at the rate of the Short Term AFR rate as published in the Wall Street Journal, per annum, and with the additional privilege of renewing the balance of said loan at its maturity, for another period of five (5) years, and the proper officers of this Company are hereby authorized and directed to sign any new or renewal note or notes required by Lender to carry out the provisions of this resolution, which new note or notes shall bear such rate of interest as shall be agreed upon between this Company and Lender at the time of such renewal or renewals.

IN WITNESS THEREOF, the undersigned have executed this written consent as of the date hereof.

DATED, this 6th day of April, 2020

_____
John Doe / Director

_____
Jane Doe / Director

Line of Credit Resolution for ABA Services, Inc.

Waiver of Notice of
Organizational Meeting for
ABA Services, Inc.
A Nevada Corporation

We the undersigned, being a majority or all of the members of the Board of Directors of ABA Services, Inc., hereby agree and consent that the Organizational Meeting of the Directors of ABA Services, Inc., be held on the date, at the location and the time stated below, for the purpose of transacting any and all business. We hereby waive all notice of the meeting and of any adjournment thereof.

Date: April 6, 2020
Location: Las Vegas,
Nevada Time: 9:00 a.m.

DATED, this 6th day of April, 2020

_____

John Doe / Director

_____

Jane Doe / Director

Waiver of Notice of Organizational Meeting
for ABA Services, Inc.

Consent to Action Without a Meeting of the Managers of ABC Investments, LLC

In accordance with the Provisions of Nevada State Law, the manager(s) identified below, constituting a majority or all of the managers of ABC Investments, LLC, hereby consents to the following action:

>   **RESOLVED** to move the Principal Office to 3225 McLeod Drive, Suite 100, Las Vegas, Nevada 89121.

A resolution for said purposes shall be adopted and appended to the minutes of this meeting.

DATED this 14th, day of March, 2020

_____

MANAGER/ **John Deaux**

_____

MANAGER / **Jane Deaux**

Minutes of the Special Meeting of Managers of ABC Investments, LLC A Duly Formed Limited Liability Company

The Special Managers Meeting of the Limited Liability Company was held at **9:00 a.m.**, on the **14th** day of **March, 2020**, at **Las Vegas, Nevada**.

The following Managers of the Limited Liability Company were present, representing a quorum:

John Deaux

Jane Deaux

John Deaux was appointed temporary Chairman and **Jane Deaux** was appointed temporary Secretary of the meeting.

The Secretary then presented and read to the meeting a Waiver of Notice of the Meeting, subscribed by all the Managers of the Limited Liability Company, and it was ordered that it be appended to the minutes of the meeting.

The Manager then rendered a general report of the business of the Limited Liability Company, also presented a report of the finances of the Limited Liability Company.

The Chairman then called for any new business.

DISCUSSED moving the Principal Office to 3225 McLeod Drive, Suite 100, Las Vegas, Nevada 89121.

There being no further business before the meeting, upon motion duly made, seconded, and carried, the meeting adjourned.

DATED this **14th** day of **March, 2020**

_____

MANAGER/ **John Deaux**

_____

MANAGER / **Jane Deaux**

The following have been appended to these minutes:

Waiver of Notice of the Special Managers Meeting

Waiver of Notice of the Special Meeting of Managers of ABC Investments, LLC A Duly Formed Limited Liability Company

We, the undersigned, being all or a majority of the Managers of ABC Investments, LLC, hereby agree and consent that the Special Meeting of the Managers of the Limited Liability Company be held on the date, at the location and the time stated below, for the purpose of transacting any and all business. We hereby waive all notice of the meeting and of any adjournment thereof.

Date: March 14, 2020
Location: Las Vegas, Nevada
Time: 9:00 AM

DATED this 14th day of March, 2020

_____

MANAGER/ **John Deaux**

_____

MANAGER / **Jane Deaux**

Minutes of the Special Meeting of Members of ABC Investments, LLC A Nevada Limited Liability Company

The Special Members Meeting of the Limited Liability Company was held at **9:30 a.m.**, on the **14th** day of **March, 2020**, at **Las Vegas, Nevada**.

The following Members of the Limited Liability Company were present, representing a quorum:

John Deaux

Jane Deaux

John Deaux was appointed temporary Chairman and temporary Secretary of the meeting.

The Secretary then presented and read to the meeting a Waiver of Notice of the Meeting, subscribed by all the Members of the Limited Liability Company, and it was ordered that it be appended to the minutes of the meeting.

The Manager then rendered a general report of the business of the Limited Liability Company, and also presented a report of the finances of the Limited Liability Company.

The Chairman then called for any new business.

DISCUSSED moving the Principal Office to 3225 McLeod Drive, Suite 100, Las Vegas, Nevada 89121.

There being no further business before the meeting, upon motion duly made, seconded, and carried, the meeting adjourned.

DATED, this **14th** day of **March, 2020**

MANAGER/ **John Deaux**

MANAGER / **Jane Deaux**

The following have been appended to these minutes:

Waiver of Notice of the Special Members Meeting

Waiver of Notice
of the Special Meeting of Members
of
ABC Investments, LLC
A Nevada Limited Liability Company

We, the undersigned, being all or a majority of the Members of **ABC Investments, LLC**, hereby agree and consent that the Special Meeting of the Members of the Limited Liability Company be held on the date, at the location and the time stated below, for the purpose of transacting any and all business. We hereby waive all notice of the meeting and of any adjournment thereof.

Date: **March 14, 2020**
Location: **Las Vegas, Nevada**
Time: **9:30 AM**

DATED, this **14th** day of **March**, 2020

_____

MANAGER/ **John Deaux**

_____

MANAGER / **Jane Deaux**

Index